Fun with Grammar

Fun with Grammar

A Workbook for All of Us

Marcielle Brandler

iUniverse, Inc.
Bloomington

Fun with Grammar
A Workbook for All of US

iUniverse books may be ordered through booksellers or by contacting:

iUniverse
1663 Liberty Drive
Bloomington, IN 47403
www.iuniverse.com
1-800-Authors (1-800-288-4677)

ISBN: 978-1-4697-7521-0 (sc)
ISBN: 978-1-4697-7522-7 (e)

Printed in the United States of America

iUniverse rev. date: 2/6/2012

Isn't it sad when bad things happen to good sentences?
—"Kate Costas, "She's the Boss" episode of *Frasier*

Contents

Acknowledgements

I would like to thank iUnverse and their staff, particularly Krista Hill and my thorough and patient editor, Jane Lusaka.

Without my students, this book would never have become a reality. It is their need for simple and concise explanations that moved me to create certain teaching techniques and the charts that have been of help to them over the years.

Many thanks my own English and Writing teachers, coaches, and professors.

I know that this book will help people all over the world understand how to write in English. I thank you in advance, and I hope this book will be a worthy guide in your journey towards improved English skills.

Welcome to Fun with Grammar

Welcome to *Fun with Grammar*, a course which I designed. As your English language mentor, I will be teaching you shortcuts to understanding the rules of the English language that will simplify and disentangle potentially confusing concepts. Remember that English is not a pure language; it is made up of English, German, Arabic, Latin, French, and Greek. So the rules may seem to change for no reason. What a mess!

Knowing that English is not just "English," means that we can be patient with ourselves. Those who are from places far from the United States will have the most intensive challenges. That is just because their languages are radically different from English. Those who speak romance languages, such as Spanish and Italian, will have less trouble, because those languages are closer to English.

Years ago, I created a class called Fun with Grammar at Pasadena City College's Extended Learning Center, where I still teach. My classes were packed with students standing outside the door asking to get in. After the first grammar class, students asked me to create a Fun with Grammar II, so I did; and now they want a Fun with Grammar III. This book contains some of those lessons. Just to give you a little example of how a person can get "unstuck" from the grammar labyrinth, let me share a story about myself.

When I was in first grade, I could not read. I had never seen a written word. My teacher told my mother that I was "retarded." My mother responded with, "Nonsense!" She took me home and taught me phonics in one hour. It was not fashionable at that time to teach phonics. The next day, my teacher moved me from Group C to Group B, and then to Group A, all in the same day! I could now sound out the words, "Run, Jane, run. See Jane run. Run, Spot, run. Run, run, run!" I will never forget that lesson.

I have watched as supposedly learning-challenged students out-perform their supposedly "normal" peers. It is all in the work, knowledge, and discipline. As students, we need to keep moving forward and not allow harmful, debilitating labels to hold us back.

I have been teaching since I was sixteen, first in my church; then when I was a housewife, I gave guitar lessons. Teaching at an Armenian school, an Orthodox Jewish yeshiva, a Korean school, several Catholic schools, including an all-black Catholic girls' high school, and many others, has given me a universal outlook, which in turn helps me deal with people's personal challenges when learning this complex language of English. As a college professor, I have taught people from Russia, the Congo, China, Guatemala, Taiwan, Sri Lanka, Armenia, Bosnia, and many other countries. They share with me many of the same problems they have with English. I am here to guide them, and you, through some of those challenges.

This is, not only a workbook, but also a book that actually *teaches* the lessons. Many of the answers have explanations to further elucidate the topics discussed. There is some repetition in this book, which is intentional. Some people may skip to a particular chapter without having seen previous information. Certain rules and concepts are repeated or stated in different formats in order to reinforce them.

I have given you numerous resources, available in hard copy and online, to enhance your language, critical thinking, and writing skills. Learning *can* be a pleasure.

Please feel free to contact me with questions or suggestions. As my students and colleagues know, I am open to your thoughts and I too am in process.

Writing Classes

Fun with Grammar I: Class Topics
Plurals and Possessives; Gerunds
The Senses; Helping and Linking Verbs
Concrete and Abstract Nouns
Subject/Object; Prepositions; Conjunctions
Spelling Rules
Commas and Other Punctuation
Major Verb Tenses
Adjectives and Adverbs; Hyphenated Modifiers

Fun with Grammar II: Class Topics
Phrases and Clauses
Who and Whom
Parallel Structure
Homonyms
Verb Practice
Word Roots
Subject/Object Review
Comparative/Superlative Adjectives

Fun with Grammar III: Class Topics
English as a Second Language (ESL) Mistakes; Time versus Place
Phrases and Clauses Review; Verb as Adjective
Number and Amount; Count and Non-count Nouns; Collective Nouns
Dividing Words into Syllables
Neither/Nor; Gerund Review
Diphthongs, Digraphs, and Tri-graphs
Synonyms, Antonyms, Vocabulary
Racist and Sexist Language; Commonly Misused Words

Writing for Everyone

Introduction

English is a strange language. We are told that the plural of *girl* is *girls*. Then, why is the plural of *man* not *mans*? If the plural of *mouse* is *mice*, then shouldn't the plural of *house* be *hice*? *Irresponsible* means not responsible, but *irrespective* has nothing to do with not being respective, and most people do not use the word *irregardless*. These variables occur, because English is composed of seven languages: English, Latin, Arabic, Greek, German, Italian, and French. Some dictionaries even say that *irregardless* is indeed a word. With all this disagreement, how can anyone decipher this varied and complex language?

This book has been created as a guide to understanding often-used phrases, tenses, grammar, punctuation, writing, and critical thinking. It does not replace comprehensive books in English grammar. I have created it as a result of my thirty-plus years of teaching. It is designed to target specific problems that we all encounter while navigating this crazy language.

I purposely put some of the exercises before the teaching part of the lesson, because I want you to actually see where your errors are. Then you will be more aware of your strengths and weaknesses in those areas before you begin the actual lesson. This strategy works very well in the classroom.

Have fun with this book. Permit yourself to make mistakes; when you correct them, you will have a better understanding of English and your relationship to it. Do not be embarrassed by an error. The error is your guide towards better understanding what you personally need to understand. I highlight my errors, so that I can be aware of them and learn the correction.

There are many resources listed in the "Works Cited" and "Suggested Resources" sections. Most of them are online; however, there are many great books available as well.

This book is laid out in sections that contain an overall discussion of each subject as well as exercises with answers that follow. The answers are often annotated so that you can grasp why one answer is correct and another incorrect. Of course, there is nothing like having a live instructor with you so that you can ask questions. I have tried to write this book as if I am sitting with you and instructing you. I use in the informal "I" when I am explaining an idea and address the reader using the informal "you" as well.

So, let's get going and have fun with grammar!

Dividing Words into Syllables

There are very specific, yet simple, rules for dividing words into syllables. When we break them, the error can be very obvious and even embarrassing.

Never divide a proper noun into syllables. For example, Mary is never Ma-ry. Try to keep the entire name on one line and definitely on the same page.

Never begin a line with a hyphen.

Incorrect

di
-vide

Correct

di-
vide

Try to divide the word as closely to the middle of the word as possible. For a long word, like unhappiness, we would break it as follows: unhappi- ness. This way, as the reader sees the beginning of the word, he knows what it is before he reaches the next line. You may divide this word anywhere that dictionaries show, but you do not want to begin with *un* and then go to the next line. It would be better to just keep the word on one line. The two spaces for *un* will not be worth it. The following is the correct way that this word can be divided into syllables: un-hap-pi-ness

Notice the *pi* in the middle of the word. Why is it not *ppi*? When the syllable has a short vowel, we usually keep the consonant next to it. We separate the double consonant.

Example: kit-tens, be-gin-ning, beg-ging, mar-ry-ing, com-mit

Syllables with *long vowels* can stand alone, almost like they need no protection. So *ba* in *babies* can stand alone, but *bies* needs that *b*.

Example: babies becomes ba-bies

If the syllable has a *short vowel*, it needs the consonant to begin it, almost like it needs protection.

Example: solitude becomes *sol-i-tude*, not so-li-tude

Never *ever* divide a *single-syllable* word (e.g., scream).

Incorrect: scre-am, cou-nt, lo-ve

When in doubt, consult a dictionary, or do not divide the word. See also the "Phonics" sections of *Free Printables for Teachers* (www.mes-english.com) and the "Works Cited" chapter of this book.

Our Different Languages

Because each language has its own personality, I want to show how the differences between a few other languages and English can cause extra problems. These differences often are made more complex, because many other languages have unique alphabets. I will mention just a few differences.

Arabic does not use pronouns like he or she.

Chinese has no verbs per se or separate letters that are combined into words. Instead, pictographs add lines for further meaning. Cantonese does not have an r sound, but Mandarin does.

In Spanish, possessive pronouns that act as adjectives, match the verb tenses.
Spanish speakers would say, "Those are mines."
In English mine, yours, ours, etc., never change.

Each non-native speaker will have his or her own unique issues when learning English. The sooner you identify your own specific issues, the faster you will improve.

Remember to be proud that you speak more than one language. You are privy to a world and consciousness that I and others, who only speak one language, are not.

Verbs

Verb Tenses
All verb types, or groups, such as *Simple, Perfect, Progressive* or *Continuous* **forms** have a present, past, and future **tense**. In this exercise, we will conjugate a regular verb and two irregular verbs in all tenses. I have included "who" in the subject list.

Simple Verb Tenses
The simple form (with its tenses) are easiest, because they deal *simply* with the present (now), past (yesterd.ay, years ago, or a minute ago), and future (any time after right now).

Subject	Present	Past	Future
I, you, we, they	walk	walked	will walk
	sleep	slept	will sleep
	bring	brought	will bring
he, she, it, who	walks	walked	will walk
	sleeps	slept	will sleep
	brings	brought	will bring

Notice that the change in endings for the future tense is always the same: *will* plus the verb.

Perfect Tenses

The *perfect form* is very difficult and requires special attention. The *past perfect* and *future perfect tenses* give students the most trouble. The *present perfect tense* is used when something has been done in the past, but not during any specific time. The *past perfect tense* is used when something has been done in the past before another time in the past. Yes, this is confusing, but keep reading and you will understand it.

The *future perfect tense* is used to indicate a time in the future that will take place *after* an earlier specific time in the future.

Subject	Present	Past	Future
I, you, we, they	have walked	had walked	will have walked
	have slept	had slept	will have slept
	have brought	had brought	will have brought
he, she, it, who	has walked	had walked	will have walked
	has slept	had slept	will have slept
	has brought	had brought	will have brought

Notice the patterns.

Present perfect
I have walked here many times before.
There is not a specific timeframe. The speaker did the walking sometime in the past and may do it again.

Past perfect
I had bought this dress before our date last night.
Notice that last night is in the past, but she'd bought the dress *before* that time. They are both in the past, but one time frame is farther in the past than the other time.

Future perfect
By the time I am twenty-five, I will have received my BA diploma.
The speaker is projecting into the future. A certain action will be done by a specific time in the future.

Perfect Continuous

The *perfect continuous tenses* combine the perfect tenses with the idea of making them ongoing. The present perfect continuous uses "have" or "has" to show that the action is ongoing, something the speaker has done in the past and will continue to do now and in the future. The past perfect continuous uses "had" to indicate that the ongoing action was over before something else in the past occurred. The future perfect continuous projects upcoming ongoing action that will be accomplished by some other subsequent time

Subject	Present	Past	Future
I, you, we, they	have been walking	had been walking	will have been walking
	have been sleeping	had been sleeping	will have been sleeping

	have been bringing	had been bringing	will have been bringing
he, she, it, who	has been walking	had been walking	will have been walking
	has been sleeping	had been sleeping	will have been sleeping
	has been bringing	had been bringing	will have been bringing

Present continuous

I have been sleeping all day.

This is an action that was happening in the past, is happening now, and may continue to happen.

Past continuous

I had been taking him food every day, but then the doctor said he could go home.

Notice that I stopped taking food when the doctor said he could go home, which was also in the past. This happens in the past before something else begins which is also in the past. It is the past *before* the past.

Future continuous

If I go to bed now, then by seven a.m. tomorrow, I will have been sleeping for ten hours.

The speaker anticipates that her sleep cycle will be completed at a specific time the following morning. This is when something will be completed by some future date.

If I start college when I am twenty and graduate when I am twenty-five, I will have been working on my BA for five years.

The *future continuous* can be used to indicate something a person is doing right now and will continue, or something he or she will begin in the future.

Progressive Tenses

Subject	Present	Past	Future
I, you, we, they	am/are walking	have been walking	will have been walking
	am/are sleeping	have been sleeping	will have been sleeping
	am/are bringing	have been bringing	will have been bringing
he, she, it, who	is/are walking	has been walking	will have been walking
	is/are sleeping	has been sleeping	will have been sleeping
	is/are bringing	has been bringing	will have been bringing

All of these tenses can be used in the negative, as in the first example below.

Examples:

A. I wish you hadn't (had not) used that brush.

B. It's (It is) for the cat.

C. If you'd (you had) asked me, I'd (would) have told you that.

D. He could if he wanted to.

E. He could, if he'd wanted to (meaning he could have done so, if he had so desired).

These two sentences suggest different things. Sentence D refers to an action in the past that could also be done in the future. Sentence E refers to the past. That action is done. It cannot be revisited. It is over.

Many students do not understand past perfect. In fact, they have an easier time with future prefect than with past perfect. A person can get by without using past perfect, but we need to understand others when they use it.

Now

Past Perfect	Past	Present	Future	Future Perfect
I had dined	I dined	I dine	I will dine	I will have dined
I had deposited. (This is finished *before* some event that also happened in the past.)	I deposited	I deposit	I will deposit	I will have deposited. (This will be finished before some event that will also happen in the future.)

Past perfect
Before I dined with my boss, I had deposited the money we made.
Both events are in the past, but one is a "done deal" by the time the other happens.

The day we had lunch, I was wearing the necklace you had given me.

Future perfect
By the time we dine this evening, I will have deposited the money we made last week.
Both events are in the future, but one will be a "done deal" by the time the other happens. The money was made before either thing will happen, so that is in the past tense.

Past perfect
I was there, because I'd received a call from an informant.
Good sentence with past tense.

She wouldn't have been hired as a nurse, if she hadn't received the training.
Good sentence with present perfect.

It doesn't seem to have rained much, so let's go hiking.
Good sentence with present tense.

I would have given you a ride home if I'd been there.
Good sentence with present perfect.

"Did she turn out as you hoped?" (from Hanna, a 2001 film).
What is wrong with the above sentence? It asks, "did she turn out," which is in the past tense and should be followed with "as you *had* hoped," which is in the past perfect tense. The hope came before she turned out a certain way. They are both in the past, but *hope* came before *turn.*

When I got to the garden, I noticed that all the roses had died.
Good sentence. The roses were dead by the time the speaker arrived.

When I got to the garden, I noticed that all the roses had been dead for at least a month.
Good sentence. Now, the speaker uses the past perfect "had been" with the adjective "dead" to indicate a time span that had occurred before her arrival.

Exercise
Cover the answers listed below. Then fill in the correct verbs.

1. By next year, I _____ learned more skills.
2. Before she learned how to drive, Mary _____ always walked to work.
3. Bill _____ hoped to be a doctor by now, but he is still in college.
4. If I hadn't dropped my bag, I _____ not _____ met you.
5. When I was hiking, I (see)_____ a huge hawk circling overhead.
6. Before I went hiking, I _____ decided to wear a hat.
7. By the time we get to the top of the mountain, it _____ rained for over an hour.
8. We _____ living in this house for ten years.
9. If she stays asleep until dinner, she _____ sleeping for more than twelve hours.

Answers
1. will have learned
2. had walked (always can be placed in the middle of the verb)
3. had hoped
4. would not have met
5. saw
6. had decided
7. had rained
8. have been living
9. will have been sleeping

Helping Verbs in Perfect Tenses (see above list)
Helping verbs have more than one word in the verb. They combine with main verbs to create a verb phrase.

Example: *have looked*

I have looked at the car.
Have is the *helping* verb and *looked* is the main verb. *Helping* verbs are also called *auxiliary* verbs. The *main* verb is also called the *principle* verb.

I will have talked to you by Thursday.
Will, *have*, and *been* are the helping verbs. *Talked* is the main verb.

In *had deposited*, *had* is the helping verb, and *deposited* is the main verb.
I dine.
There is only one word in the verb and that is the main verb, *dine*, so there is no helping verb in this sentence. In *will dine*, *will* is the helping verb, and *dine* is the main verb.

Exercise
Write five sentences using helping verbs. Discuss.

Simple Past Tense: Pronunciation of Verbs
Pronounce the *ed* like a *t* or a strong *d*. It must be sounded in order to indicate that it is the past and not the present, that it already happened.

I bak*ed* a cake (*t* sound).
She brush*ed* her hair (*t* sound).
Jason climb*ed* a hill (*d* sound).
The dog bark*ed* (*t* sound).
We lock*ed* the door last night (*t* sound).
The students failed the test yesterday (*d* sound).

Verbs as Adjectives
Sometimes, verbs can act as adjectives. We usually think of words like *failed, excited, locked, stripped, degraded,* and *spoiled* as verbs. Such as: The food has spoiled. The below sentences use these verbs as adjectives.

He is a *failed* businessman.
She is an *excited* girl.
We are behind *locked* doors.
The *stripped* wood of the table has been refinished.
She felt *degraded.*
It smells *spoiled.*

Exercise
Write sentences using these verbs as adjectives:
1. depress
2. cancel
3. add

Contrary to Fact

Contrary to fact indicates that the idea is not true. You should use *were* instead of *are* or *is.* Bob should not say, "I wish I *was* a better baseball player," but "I wish I *were* a better baseball player," because he is not a better player.

Use the word *were* to indicate that a wish, hope, or action, is contrary to fact.

Examples:
If I <u>were</u> to own a Rolls Royce, I would drive it on Sundays.
This is because I do not own a Rolls Royce.

If I <u>am</u> to own a Rolls Royce ... means I intend to own one in the future.

She acts as if she <u>were</u> the queen of Sheba.
She is not the queen.

If I <u>were</u> you, I would study more.
The person speaking is not the *you* to whom he speaks.

Exercise
Write five sentences using "contrary to fact" ideas. Discuss.

"Before You Learn" Exercise

Cover the answer chart below. Circle the correct option in the sentences before you look at the chart. See what you already know, so that you can track your progress after the lesson.

1. Bob was nice to everyone except Mary and (she/her).
2. Everyone except Carolyn and (he/him) went to the party.
3. Charles and (he/him) went to the party.
4. Can you talk to Jennifer and (they/them)?
5. Manny and (they/them) would like to join us.
6. A producer will buy a script if (they/she) think/s it will make money.
7. (Who/Whom) are you going to choose as the winner?
8. It was (she/her) who went with Bob.
9. Dustin Hoffman, one of the best actors alive, did (their/his) best work in *Rain Man*.

Answers

1. *Her.* Except is a preposition that signals that Mary and her are both objects.
2. *Him.*
3. *He* went.
4. Can you talk to *them*? Leave Jennifer out of the sentence. Focus only on subject, verb, and object. That is a little trick.
5. *They* would like to join. Forget about Manny for now.
6. *She.* A producer is only one person. You might think of producers only as men, and that is where you can get into trouble.
7. *Whom.* You are choosing the person. You are choosing *him* or *whom*. Explained in greater detail below.
8. *She* was the one who did it. *She* is the same as *it*. It was she. She was it. It is like *she* is the subject of the sentence twice.
9. *His.* Watch out for interruptions in the sentence that can confuse you. Notice the commas around the adjectival phrase, which describes Hoffman.

Who versus Whom

To figure when to use *who* and *whom*, replace *who* with *he* and *whom* with *him* in the sentence. For example, see number 7 above: Who/whom are you going to choose as the winner? You are going to choose *him* because *you* are doing the choosing. The *him* is the object who is acted upon, as is the *whom*. *Him* and *whom* are always objects of sentences. *He* and *who* are always subjects; the ones who *do* or who *are*. See the "Subject/Object" chart in this book for guidance.

The *subject* of the sentence is the one who *does* or who *is*. It is in the nominative case. You can think of it in this way: the person nominates to do or to be. That person creates the action or is just being there. We would never say "Me am walking" or "Me am happy," because the *me* should be *I*.

The *object* of the sentence receives the action, meaning that *it*, *he*, or *she* is acted upon, and each one is in the *objective* case. You would not say, "Bob said hello to I," because *I* should be *me*. *Me* is in the objective case.

Subject/Object Chart

The "Subject/Object Chart" is my own creation and cannot be found in other sources. Notice that the subject is the main person in the sentence. A sentence does not always have an object (i.e., the one who receives the action or thought created by the subject). The object does not do anything. The object is acted upon. *You* and *it* are in parentheses, because they do not change from the subjective to the objective case.

Subject	Verb	Preposition	Object
Nominative case: one who does or is; creates the action			**Objective case: one to whom something is done; receives the action**
		on, under, through, until, during, before, except, while	
I (you) we they	said hello thought laughed talked	to about at with	me (you) us them
he she (it) who		within, inside, below, since, without, throughout	him her (it) whom

Subject/Object Error

Object error
"Do you think you can make Clark and I trust you again?"–
—Lois in the "Ambush" episode of *Smallville*, 2010
Say to yourself, "Do you think *you can make me* trust you?" and you will understand. Forget about Clark (i.e., the other person [object] mentioned in the sentence). Isolate the object, and you will get it every time.

Incorrect: "I would make her and I this huge Easter basket."
Correct: I would make an Easter basket for her and me.

Subject Error
Incorrect:
Me and him were there.
This is a very bad error.

Correct:
He and I were there.
Say, "I was there," and "he was there." You would not say, "Him was there," or "Me was there."

Exercise
Write the three sentences with misused words, and then three sentences with the errors corrected. Discuss.

Prepositions

Prepositions join subjects to objects. A preposition usually will be followed by an object, but not always (e.g., *to* the store, *on* the couch, *in* my hand, *over* the land, *throughout* her day, *except* them, *during* the storm, etc). "Mary saw Bob" does not have a preposition. Mary is the subject; Bob is the object. However, "Mary looked at Bob" has the preposition *at*.

Examine the above Subject/Object chart for patterns and more prepositions.Read the above paragraph above before completing the exercise below.

Subject/Object/Preposition Exercise
Cover the answers below. Then circle the correct answers. Place a box around the preposition and underline the prepositional phrase. Number one has been done for you.

1. Julie, Donna, and (her/**she**) will be **at** rehearsal.
2. Did the professor ask Dave, Bob, and (she/her) to come to his office?
3. They sat between Ahmad and (I/me).
4. They and (we/us) are having a great time.
5. Everyone except (she/her) went to the party.
6. It was (I/me) who paid the bill.
7. I love to watch a great actress, who is better than most actresses, doing (their/her) best work.
8. You can find information about Dustin, Tom, and (she/her) on the Internet.
9. Dustin, Tom, and (she/her) will appear in more films.
10. I watched Dustin, Tom, and (she/her) in many films.

Answers The prepositions are in **bold** print.
1. she / **at** rehearsal
2. her / **to** his office
3. me / **between** Ahmad and me.
4. we No prepositional phrase
5. her / **to** the party
6. I / No prepositional phrase
7. her / No prepositional phrase
8. her / **on** the Internet
9. she / **in** more films
10. her/ **in** many films

Ending Sentences with Prepositions

The phrase, "to that which you are referring to," is redundant in that it uses *to* twice, and it also ends with a preposition. Sometimes in speech, we cannot avoid doing it. You might say "I would like to," but write, "I would like to do that." In speech, we take shortcuts. *The Chicago Manual of Style* says that ending a sentence with a preposition is now acceptable. See how the language changes? When I write formal pieces, I continue to be conservative and avoid ending sentences with prepositions. Below are examples of what I still consider to be incorrect. Make your own decisions as how to write.

Examples:
Incorrect:
She is the one he is looking at.

Correct:
She is the one at whom he is looking.
To avoid this very formal-sounding structure, say, "He is looking at her."

Incorrect:
What did you buy that for?

Correct:
For what reason did you buy that?
Why did you buy that?

Indefinite Pronouns

Indefinite pronouns can be subjects or objects, but there are a few challenges associated with them.

Circle the subject of the following sentence:
Each of the girls (is/ are) here.

Remember that there has to be subject/verb agreement. If you circled *are*, that means you think the subject is *girls*. If you circled *is*, then you think the subject is *each*, which is correct. *Of the girls* is an adjectival phrase or a *modifier*, that describes *each*. Each what? Each of the girls. Each is a *singular indefinite pronoun* and is the subject of the sentence, so you should say, *Each is*. Each (*one* understood) is.

Exercise
Underline the subject to help you identify the verb that should agree with (match) it.

1. Many of my friends (has/have) good financial portfolios.
2. One of the people in my group (is a /are) millionaire/s.
3. None of them (is/are) selfish.
4. Marineh's friend was one of the people who earned (their/her) degree at UCLA.
5. Neither of my two best friends (is/are) very tall.

Answers
1. Many *have*
2. One *is*
3. None *is* (this is singular, meaning not one or no one)
4. Friend requires *her*
5. Neither *is* (one is understood, as in neither one)

Neither/Nor: "Before You Learn" Exercise
Cover the answers below; then circle the correct options in the following:

1. Neither Candace nor Samantha (have/has) an Acura.
2. Neither the boys nor Mr. Smith (have/has) the money.
3. Either Mr. Smith or the boys (have/has) the money.

Whatever comes after "or" or "nor" is the noun to choose. In number 1, *Samantha* comes after *nor*, and requires *has*. In number 2, Mr. Smith comes after *nor*, which is singular and requires *has*. Mr. Smith *has* …

Answers
1. Samantha *has*
2. Mr. Smith *has*
3. The boys *have*

Now, try again.

"After You Have Learned" Exercise
1. Neither Mr. Smith nor the boys (have/has) the money.
2. Neither you nor I (is/am) allowed in this room.
3. Neither Carey nor the swimmers (is/are) allowed in the pool.
4. Either they or he (climb/climbs) onto the roof to get the ball.

Answers
1. the boys have
2. I am
3. swimmers are
4. he climbs

Indefinite Pronouns List

Singular	Plural
one	many
neither	some
either	all
every	several
each	both

Exercise
Write three sentences using singular indefinite pronouns and three with plural indefinite pronouns. Discuss.

Any English book or website will have a complete list of indefinite pronouns.

Linking Verbs

Linking verbs connect nouns to their descriptions (modifiers or adjectives).

Noun = description
Dawn = intelligent.
Dawn is intelligent. *Is* links *Dawn* to *intelligent.*

Ahmad = hardworking.
Ahmad seems hardworking. *Seems* links *Ahmad* to *hardworking.*

You never say *I am me,* just like you would not say *Me is I.* The *I* person is the subject of the sentence and is the same person as himself, so nothing is happening to, for, or at him. He is just being himself. He is not an object but is the subject twice.

I am I.
This is I.
I am this.

Examples of linking verbs: *am, are, is, will be, feel, look, smell*

You look well.
This sentences means that you are well. You *look* beautiful, meaning that your looks are (you are) beautiful. You = beautiful.

The word look also can indicate an action, such as, you *look* at the desk. In this case, it would not be a linking verb.

I feel ill.
In this sentence feel is a linking verb that indicates "I *am* ill." "Am" is a form of the verb "to be." Linking verbs are a state of being, not doing.

The word *feel* can be an action, such as I *feel* (handle or touch) the soft cloth, or I *feel* (touch) the table. In this case, it would not be a linking verb but an action verb.

This meat smells rancid.
"Smells" is a linking verb

I like to smell the flowers.
"Smell" is an action verb.

Exercise
Write three sentences using the examples above. First, make them linking verbs, and then action verbs.

Lie/Lay/Tell a Lie
The "Lie/Lay/Tell a Lie" chart gives a clear picture of how these verbs can be used incorrectly. The past tense of lie, which is *lay,* is the same as the present tense of lay.

	Present	Past	Future	Past Participle = Present Perfect	Present Progressive
Lie = recline. Lie down.					
I (you)	lie	lay	will lie	have lain	am/is lying
we, they					are lying
he, she, (it), who	lies	lay	will lie	has lain	is lying
Lay = to put something down.					
I, (you), we, they	lay	laid	will lay	have laid	am/are laying
he, she, (it), who	lays	laid	will lay	has laid	is laying
Notice that the past tense of *lie* is *lay*, which is the same as the present tense of *lay*. Some people say *have laid*, when they should say *have lain*, the present perfect of *lie*.					
To lie = to tell an untruth.					
I, (you), we they	lie	lied	will lie	have lied	am/are lying
he, she, (it), who	lies	lied	will lie	has lied	is lying

Exercise

Cover the answers below. Fill in the blank with the correct form of the verbs *lie* or *lay*.

1. I always _____ my book on the same table when I come home.
2. I always _____ down for a nap when I get home.
3. Why do you always _____ around, instead of helping us clean up?
4. Please help me _____ the fire.
5. I _____ under this tree many times.
6. Will Joshua help _____ the table for dinner?
7. I just _____ my flute in its box.
8. Now that I _____ the flute safely in its case, I can close the lid.
9. My dad _____ down the law with all of us children.
10. Please start by _____ your papers in front of you.

Answers

1. lay
2. lie
3. lie
4. lay
5. have lain
6. lay
7. laid
8. have laid

9. laid
10. laying

Nouns

Abstract and Concrete Nouns

We think of a noun as a *person, place,* or *thing.* That is true, but some of our teachers forgot to tell us that a nouns is also a non-physical "thing."

Abstract nouns include ideas, emotions, belief systems, and other intangible concepts, but since we cannot perceive them with the six senses, they are difficult to identify.

Concrete nouns are those things we can see, hear, touch, taste, and smell. They exist in the physical world, often right in front of us, and because of this, we can more easily identify them. The chart below will help you understand more clearly. It is designed to break down the different kinds of nouns into their largest groups. This chart is my own creation and cannot be found in other sources.

Common nouns are simply nouns that are not a proper nouns, which are names and are capitalized, nor are they pronouns, like *she* or *he*. *Girl, magnet, chair,* and *cloud* are all common nouns.

Pronouns stand for the person, place, thing, or idea being mentioned in the sentence, so that regular nouns do not have to be repeated. They take the place of the original nouns (the antecedents). *She* and *her* both stand for the common noun *girl.* See the "Pronouns and Antecedents" section below.

Proper nouns are always capitalized, because they are the names of people, places, things, and ideas. The name, *Madeline* stands for a specific girl, so *Madeline* is a proper noun. The word, *philosophy* is a common noun, but *Existentialism,* which is a specific philosophy, is capitalized.

		Common	*Pronoun*	*Proper*
C O	Person	girl	she, her	Madeline
		president	he, him	Abraham Lincoln
N	Place	city	it	Budapest
C R E T E	Thing	chair	it	Chippendale
		tiger	it, he, she	Bengal tiger
		house	it	White House
		school	it	El Monte High School

A	Idea		it	Mesozoic Era
B S	Feeling	emotions, love, hatred	it, them	

		creativity, philosophy, inquiry, statements, conversation	it, them	Communism, Catholicism, Buddhism
T R				
A C		authorship, subjects, mathematics, college course	It, them,	Math 101, University of Southern California
T		celebration, calculations, resourcefulness, kindness	it, them	Martin Luther King Jr. Day is a celebration
		distance, closeness, loudness, traits, theory	it, them	Maslow's Hierarchy of Needs is a theroy

To make abstract ideas more concrete, create examples using the five senses: taste, see, hear, touch, and smell.

If I want to make you understand how stinky the laundry room is, I might say:
The smell of mildew punched me in the face and rushed into my nostrils like a gust of baby diaper pooh.

The fact that I am *punched in the face*, is an assault. *Baby diaper pooh* is something we all know, and its odor is very strong. This is better than just saying the laundry room stinks.

Exercise
Cover the answers below. Put A next to abstract nouns, and C next to concrete nouns.

1. __ discrimination
2. __ dynamite
3. __ a fight
4. __ peace
5. __ piece of cake
6. __ piece of my mind
7. __ disappointment
8. __ hiking path
9. __ life's path
10. __ squeamishness
11. __ library
12. __ goal in life
13. __ absence
14. __ prize
15. __ a thought
16. __ inventor
17. __ constancy
18. __ mentality
19. __ anger
20. __ medicine
21. __ nationality
22. __ who
23. __ card

Answers

1. A 2. C 3. A 4. A 5. C 6. A 7. A 8. C 9. A 10. A 11. C 12. A
13. A 14. C 15. A 16. C 17. A 18. A 19. A 20. C 21. A 22. C 23. C

Exercise

Use five or more of the above words in simple sentences; then rewrite those sentences in a way that makes the senses come alive. In other words, turn the abstractions into concrete ideas. Have fun with this. Discuss.

Describe a room, park, neighborhood, campus, business, person, group, galaxy, ecosystem, bodily function, belief system, lifestyle, food, or any other abstract thing using at least three of the senses.

Pronouns and Antecedents

A pronoun works in place of the original noun in order to avoid repetition, and so we can avoid sentences like this: Monica went to Monica's room, took out Monica's (her) favorite dress and ironed Monica's dress (it).

Pronouns are used in place of their antecedents (ante = before; cedent = go. The antecedent goes before the pronoun.

The boy lost his baseball.
Boy is the antecedent; *his* is the (possessive) pronoun.

Pronouns in the subjective case: I, you, we, they, he, she, it, who.
Pronouns in the objective case: me, you, us, them, him, her, it, whom.

See also the section on "Relative Pronouns" and the "Subject/Object Chart."

Personal Pronouns

A personal pronoun stands in place of the person's name or description. *Man* becomes *him* or *he*. *Chair* becomes *it*.

Incorrect:
The man walked into the store, bought the man's favorite pie, and then paid the man's bill.

Correct:
The man walked into the store, bought *his* favorite pie, and then paid *his* bill.

His/Her

We no longer have to use "he/she," "him/her," of "his/her" when referring to nonspecific individuals. It is acceptable to choose one and use that in one paragraph; then, use the other in the next paragraph or stay with the same one with which we began, although it is often best to use just one for the sake of consistency and to avoid confusion.

When studying, the student should not turn on her TV, radio, or any other device. She should focus only on her work.

It is very awkward to say: *When studying, the student should not turn on his/her TV, radio, or any other device. He/she should focus only on his/her work.*

Exercise
Write four sentences using *he/she*. Then write four using *he* and four using *she*.
Notice the differences between the sentences.

Possessive Pronouns
Possessive pronouns show ownership using the following words: *his, hers, mine, yours, ours, theirs, its, whose*. Notice that these nouns do not use apostrophes to show possession.

Exercise
Write one sentence for each of the possessive pronouns listed above.
Example: *I lost **my** USB drive.*

Gerunds

Complete the exercise below to see how well you understand gerunds.

"Before You Learn" Exercise
Cover the answers below; then circle the answers you believe are correct.

1. (Me/My) having this headache will not stop me from doing my work.
2. We were irritated by (him/his) being late.
3. Mom was worried about (us/our) going for a hike, so we went to the arboretum.
4. Did they see (him/his) acting?
5. Did you notice (everyone's/everyone) trying so hard to win?
6. Mom was concerned about (him/his) finishing his homework.

Answers
Adding *ing* often makes a verb become a noun; this is called a gerund. It belongs to the person mentioned.

1. *My* having this headache will not stop me from doing my work. You can also say, *My headache* will not stop me from doing my work. You would never say, *Me* having this headache. "Me" is never the subject of any sentence. Refer to the "Subject/Object Chart" in this book for more information.

2. *his* being late. You could also say "his lateness" or "his tardiness." *We were irritated by his being late. Mary was irritated by his constant tardiness.*

3. *our* going for a hike. Mom was worried about our going for a hike. To say, "Mom was worried about our hike" sounds like the speaker is worried about the hike rather than the hikers.

4. *his* acting. Did they see his acting? *Acting* serves as a noun   and belongs to the man.

5. *everyone's* trying. You could also say "everyone's effort."

6. *his* finishing. Mom is not concerned about him. She is concerned about his *finishing*.

Gerunds are *verbs* that become nouns and belong to the person in the sentence.

My little trick:

When I am trying to figure out whether a word is a gerund, I replace it with a noun that is very obviously a noun. I may write the below sentence, then consider a few thoughts.

Example: She didn't like him laughing. I ask myself, "What word, *that **is** a noun*, would work in the place of *laughing*?" How about laughter? Laughter is, for sure, a noun. Let's try it. She didn't like his laughing. Yes, that works.

The reason we get confused, is that we think, "She didn't like him (as he was) laughing. But the problem is that it means that she didn't like him, period. It does not really work in correct English. It is his *laughter or laughing* that she didn't like.

Example: The students were disturbed by him entering late. The word *entrance* is a noun. I could say, "The students were disturbed by his late entrance." I can change it to, "The students were disturbed by his entering late." Both sentences work, but the latter is the gerund.

Exercise

Now that you understand more, try using gerunds again:

1. I cannot stand (him/his) snoring all night.
2. Are you aware of (us/our) entering your garden?
3. Where did they see (us/our) dancing?
4. Can she smell (us/our) cooking?

Answers

1. his
2. our
3. us and our (you can say it both ways)
4. our

Plural Nouns

See the chapter on Nouns. This section precedes the section on Possessives, so that students have a direct link between the singular, plural, and possessive forms of the same words in the lists below.

Plural just means more than one. Singular means one. Ex: One *dog* is singular. Two *dogs* is plural,

Exercise

Write the plurals of the below nouns. First, cover the answers below to see how well you can do.

Singular	*Plural*
1. girl	_____
2. child	_____
3. wolf	_____
4. church	_____
5. waltz	_____

6. Parks   _____
7. Kennedy   _____
8. princess   _____
9. Martinez   _____
10. receipt   _____
11. baby   _____
12. piano   _____
13. tomato   _____
14. calf   _____
15. cupful   _____
16. sister-in-law _____
17. attorney   _____
18. earnings   _____
19. tooth   _____
20. quarrel   _____
21. attorney general _____
22. radio   _____
23. echo   _____

Answers
1. girls
2. children
3. wolves
4. churches
5. waltzes
6. Parkses
7. Kennedys
8. princesses
9. Martinezes
10. receipts
11. babies
12. pianos
13. tomatoes
14. calves
15. cupfuls
16. sisters-in-law
17. attorneys
18. earnings
19. teeth
20. quarrels
21. attorneys general
22. radios
23. echoes

The Rules for Plurals
Words ending in *ch, sh, x, z, s,* or *ss* use an *es* ending. See examples above.

Many foreign words that end in *o*, especially those of Italian origin, use an *s* ending. Words that are musical fit into this category, like *soprano, basso, and alto*. So do *radio* and *silo, and kimonos*.

If it ends in *o* and is preceded by a vowel, add *s* (e.g., *patio, stereo*, and *shampoo*).

Other words that end in *o,* use an *es* ending (e.g., *hero, potato*, and *halo*).

When a word ends in a *y* that is preceded by a consonant, change the *y* to *i* and then add *es*. Thus, *baby* becomes *babies*.

When a word ends in a *y* preceded by a vowel, put *s* on the end, as in *attorneys*. Proper nouns, like *Kennedy*, cannot be changed; thus, *Kennedies* is incorrect. *Emmy* must be *Emmys*, not *Emmies*. But add *es* to the end of a proper noun ending in *s* or *z*, as in *Parks (Parkses)* and *Martinez (Martinezes)*, to make the plurals.

The plural forms of words that end in *lf, f,* or *fe* are made with *ves*, as in *calves* and *wolves*. Exceptions: *safe, belief, roof, sheriff*, and *chief*, which add *s* to make the plurals.

Child (which is from the Middle and Old English) becomes *children*.

Some words stay the same in both singular and plural forms, such as *moose, deer, trout, fish* (although *fishes* can be used poetically).

Examples of words that are always plural in form are *athletics, scissors*, and *thanks*.

Exercise
Write three words that always take the plural form. Some answers are suggested below.
1. _____
2. _____
3. _____

Answers
civics, economics, mathematics, pants, trousers

Possessives of Nouns

To spell possessives correctly, it is necessary to know how to make the plurals of nouns. That is why it is important that we complete the previous exercise on plurals before we do the below exercise.

Exercise
Make the nouns below possessive. An example of a possessive noun appears in the following sentence: *That cat's eyes are like mirrors.*
The eyes belong to the cat; thus *cat's* is in the possessive form.

Do not be discouraged if you do not know how to make possessives. They do not exist in most other languages the way they do in English.

Possessives

Singular	*Plural*
1. girl	_____
2. child	_____
3. wolf	_____
4. church	_____
5. waltz	_____
6. Jones	_____
7. Anthony	_____
8. princess	_____
9. Jimenez	_____
10. receipt	_____
11. baby	_____
12. piano	_____
13. tomato	_____
14. calf	_____
15. cupful	_____
16. sister-in-law	_____
17. attorney	_____
18. earnings	_____
19. tooth	_____
20. quarrel	_____
21. attorney general	_____
22. radio	_____
23. echo	_____

The same nouns were used in the "Plural Nouns" section. Notice that certain patterns appear with these words.

Answers

Singular	*Plural*
1. girl's	girls'
2. child's	children's
3. wolf's	wolves'
4. church's	churches'
5. waltz's	waltzes'
6. Jones's	Joneses'
7. Anthony's	Anthonys'
8. princess's	princesses'
9. Jimenez's	Jimenezes'
10. receipt's	receipts'
11. baby's	babies'
12. piano's	pianos'
13. tomato's	tomatoes'
14. calf's	calves'
15. cupful's	cupfuls'

16. sister-in-law's — sisters-in-law's
17. attorney's — attorneys'
18. earnings' — earnings'
19. tooth's — teeth's
20. quarrel's — quarrels'
21. attorney general's — attorneys general's
22. radio's — radios'
23. echo's — echoes'

The Rules for Possessives

The rules are more complicated than many of us may realize. We were taught that if the word is singular like *girl*, then just add *'s* to make it possessive and *s'* to make it plural possessive. That is true only for regular nouns.

1. First, decide if the word is singular or plural, and write it as such. Make sure you spell it correctly. This example uses a regular, irregular, and proper noun with two syllables and a proper noun with three syllables.

dog	dogs	mothers-in-law	Dickenses	Anderson
singular	*plural*	*plural*	*plural*	*singular*

2. Then, decide whether to add an *apostrophe s ('s)* or *s apostrophe (s')*.

dog's	dogs'	mothers-in-law's	Dickenses'	Anderson's
singular	*plural*	*plural*	*plural*	*singular*

Because *dog* is a regular noun, follow the rule and add *'s* for the singular and *s'* for the plural. Easy. With *mothers-in-law* (just as with *children* and *wolves*), the plural is already built into the word. But here is the trick: Treat it like a singular noun, and just add *'s*. That is all!

3. Consider how many syllables the word has. For Dickenses, we added *es* to make the plural, which is more than one Dickens. It already has three syllables, so we cannot afford to make the word longer by adding *'s*, so just add the apostrophe. There is already an *s* at the end of the word, so we do not need to add one.

Anderson has three syllables, but *'s* will not make it sound like it has four syllables. The possessive plural of *Anderson* is *Andersons'*, which is still three syllables. Because Anderson, in its singular form, does not have an *s* at the end, we need to add one.

Who and Whom

The cat, (who/whom) I think is female, is sleeping on our porch.
How do we figure out whether to use *who* or *whom*? Notice the commas before and after *I think is female*. This clause is separated from the rest of the sentence. It interrupts the sentence, but it does not change the fact that the cat is the female one.

When you look at the "Subject/Object chart" in this book, you see that you can think of the cat is the subject of the sentence. . *She* is in the Nominative case. *Who* is also in the Nominative case. Just as you would say, *She is female*, so you would also say, *who is female*. These are both in the Nominative case of the noun. If you said, *whom is female*, it would be like saying *her is female*, because *whom* and *her* are in the Objective case and would be objects of the sentence. So the answer is *who*.

The cat, (who whom) is sleeping on our porch, lost an ear.
Who is doing the sleeping? The cat. So you could say, *He* is sleeping, right? When you look at the "Subject/Object chart" in this book, you see that *he* is in the Nominative case, *because he* is doing the action, just as *who* is in the Nominative case, because *who* is doing the sleeping.

My little trick:
Who is in the nominative (active) case. When I am trying to figure out *who* and *whom*, I replace them with *he* (subject) and *him* (object) to help me. Now I know that it must be *who*. I do that because *who* has a vowel at the end of the word, like *he* (They are in the nominative case) and *whom* has an *m* at the end of the word like *him* (They are in the objective case).

Incorrect:
Him is sleeping on our porch (object). *Whom* is sleeping on our porch?

Correct:
He is sleeping on our porch (subject). *Who* is sleeping on our porch?

Incorrect: I saw *he* sleeping. *Who* did I see sleeping?

Correct:
Did I see *him* sleeping? *Whom* did I see sleeping?

Exercise
Now, you try it. First, cover the answers below.

1. My aunt is the one (who/whom) is president of her club.
2. (Who/Whom) should I say is calling?
3. (Who/Whom) is calling?
4. To (who/whom) are you giving this money?
5. (Who/Whom) do you call when you need someone to confide in?
6. In (who/whom) do you confide?
7. I don't know (who/whom) told you that.
8. She was the one to (who/whom) the policeman was speaking.
9. (Who/Whom) do you see when you need counseling?
10. I cannot decide (who/whom) to reward for this.
11. I cannot decide (who/whom) should be rewarded for this.

Answers
1. Who. *She* (who) is president
2. Who is calling. "Should I say" is a separate clause.
3. Who.
4. Whom. You are giving the money to *him* (whom).
5. Whom. Whom do you call? You call *him*.
6. Whom. You confide in *him* (whom).

7. Who. *He* (who) told; not *him* (whom) told.
8. Whom. The policeman was speaking *to her*, not *to she*.
9. Whom. You see *him* (whom).
10. Whom. *Him*. I should reward him.
11. Who. He should be rewarded.

Whoever and Whomever

"Before You Learn" Exercise

Do the exercise before reading the lesson to see what you already understand. Begin by covering the answers below.

1. The policeman arrested (whoever/whomever) was running away.
2. (Whoever/Whomever) they felt looked guilty would be booked.
3. The detectives questioned (whoever/whomever) they suspected of a crime
4. The woman said, "(Whoever/Whomever) is my future mate, will be at this party."
5. She said, "I want to meet (whoever/whomever).
6. (Whoever/Whomever) paid that lady's bill should be rewarded.

This is like *who and whom* but the correct pronoun is determined within its own section (clause) in the sentence. Use *he* and *him* as your guide if you need to. It has helped many other students and even this author.

For number 1, it says, "The policeman arrested (whoever/whomever) was running away."

My little trick:
When you are figuring whoever and whomever, you just consider the part where whoever/whomever shows up. Only think about, "whoever/whomever was running away." If the person *is in the nominative case* and is *doing or being the action or thing,* then it is *whoever (he).* If the person *is the object and is just being acted upon*, then it is *whomever (him).*

Answers

1. Whoever. *He* (whoever) was running. You would not say him was running or whomever was running.
2. Whoever. *He* (whoever) looked guilty.
3. Whomever. They suspected *him* (whomever).
4. Whoever is. *He* is.
5. Whom. I want to meet *him* (whomever).
6. Whoever. *He* (whoever) paid.

Whose/Who's

Exercise

Complete this exercise before reading the lesson below.

1. She's the one (whose/who's) always on time.

2. (Whose/Who's) wallet is this?
3. (Whose/Who's) going to get the pizza?
4. (Whose/Who's) grades are the highest?

Answers
1. Who's (who is).
2. Whose (belongs to whom).
3. Who's (who is).
4. Whose (belongs to whom).

Whose is a possessive pronoun, like *his, mine, yours, ours*, and *theirs*. (See "Possessive Pronouns" in this book.) We usually use *whose* when we ask a question about something belonging to someone we cannot identify.

Example: Whose book is that? That book is mine.

Who's is a contraction of *who is* or *who has*.
Who's coming over? Who is coming over?
Who's got a camera we can use? Who has got a camera we can use? This is an awkward sentence, but people speak like this. *Has got* is the awkward part. A more eloquent sentence would be, Who has a camera we can use?

Time versus Place

Incorrect:
"It was a *time where* women could not vote." *Time* is not a place. The correct way to say this is: "It was a time *when* ..." or "It was a time *during which* ...."

Other Errors

Never say, "I met this special guy." *This* means he is right here.

Guy is slang for man, so say *man* instead. Say,"I met a man. Guy is also a French man's name, pronounced in English like "gie," and pronounced in French like "Gee"

Do not use *really* as an adverb to modify *special guy*. Say *very* or *extremely*. *Really* means that it actually happened. Everyone, even teachers, uses this word to mean *very*. Merriam-Webster says that using *really* is acceptable, but that does not make it eloquent.

Exercise
Rewrite these sentences using the above instructions as a guide. Cover the answers below.

1. I remember a time where our teachers were very strict.
2. There was this girl who made beautiful sweaters.
3. I met this really cute guy at the mall.

4. I drove this really amazing car!

Answers
1. when
2. a girl *This* girl means that she is right next to you.
3. I met a very handsome man or a cute man
4. an amazing car

Homonyms

Homo means "same"; *nym* mean "name." Thus, *homonym* means "same name." Homonyms are words that sound the same but are spelled differently and have different meanings.

Exercise
Write as many words with the same sound as possible, including proper nouns, even though they may not be considered homonyms. Then look at the list below. Words in parentheses are definitions.

1. roll, role
2. gym, Jim (slightly different sounding)
3. leak, leek
4. morning, mourning
5. steal, steel
6. flee, flea
7. horse, hoarse
8. real, reel
9. fair, fare
10. poor, pour, pore
11. peek, peak, pique
12. soul, sole
13 stair, stare
14. blare, Blair
15. rain, rein, reign
16. ware, wear, where
17. course, coarse
18. need, knead
19. read, reed, Reid
20. weather, whether
21. raise, raze
22. bear, bare
23. hurts, hertz
24. straight, strait
25. plain, plane
26. leak, leek
27. week, weak

28. principle, principal
29. peel, peal
30. capital, capitol
31. ferry, fairy
32. hawk, hock (to pawn)
33. marry, merry, Mary
34. wreak, reek
35. site, sight, cite
36. in, inn
37. sign, sine (wave)
38. medal, metal, mettle (courage)
39. would, wood
40. canvas, canvass (campaign)
41. whole, hole
42. holy, wholly (entirely)
43. pea, pee
44. born, borne (transported)
45. shoot, chute
46. hay, hey, Haye
47. click, clique
48. wet, whet
49. peace, piece
50. pole, poll Pole (as in Polish)

Synonyms and Antonyms

Synonyms

Syno means "similar"; *nym* means "name." Synonyms are words that mean the same things. They do not have to sound alike. *Love* and *adore* mean the same thing. They are synonyms.

Below are some synonyms:
hateful   despicable
right   correct

Exercise

List five synonyms. Discuss them. Use a dictionary or thesaurus if necessary.

Antonyms

Anto means "other"; *nym* means "name." Antonyms are words that have opposite meanings. *Love* is the antonym of *hatred*.

Below are some antonyms
above   below
right   left
silence   noise

29

Exercise

List five antonyms. Discuss them. Use a dictionary or thesaurus if necessary.

Common Language Problems

Incorrect:

She put <u>up</u> Arnold's briefcase, put his heavy books <u>on</u> the <u>swing up</u> table, and rested.

Correct:

She put <u>away</u> Arnold's briefcase, put his heavy books <u>on</u> the <u>swing-up</u> table, and rested.

She put the books on a *swing-up table*, not a swing.

Sometimes we use a verb when we should use its noun form. Below are a few examples.

Verb	*Noun*
to orient	orientation
to plead	a plea
to hate	**hatred (This is so common that it has become the norm.)**
to quote	**a quotation (This is so common that it has become the norm.)**

Diphthongs, Digraphs, and Trigraphs

A Digraph is *any two letters* joined together to make one sound, like the *ph* in *phonics*.
A Diphthong is the sound a digraph makes which is composed of two *vowels* joined together to make one sound, like the *oy* in *boy*.
A Trigraph is a three-letter combination that makes one sound, like the *eau* in *beauty*.

Diphthongs

Diphthongs are the *sounds* that a combination of two letters make.

Vowel Diphthongs

A vowel diphthong is the blending of two vowels sounds; both vowel sounds are usually heard, and they make a gliding sound. Examples include:

oi, as in boil
oy, as in toy
au, as in haul
aw, as in saw
ew, as in new
ow, as in cow
oo, as in moon
oo, as in look
ou, as in mouth.

-The above examples are from *PhonicsWorld.com*.

Exercise
Create five words using vowel diphthongs.

Digraphs are letter combinations that cannot be split from one another. Together, they create a certain sound.

Consonant Digraphs
A consonant digraph combines two consonants to make one sound.
gh can make an *f* sound, as in *laugh*.
gh is silent in *though*, which sounds like "tho."

There are two *th* sounds. Persian friends and students need to practice these two sounds.
th = *the, this*
th = *thought, thank*

Other consonant digraphs are: sh, ch, wh, ck, ph.
-The above examples are from *PhonicsWorld.com*.

In the word "ascend," the *sc* creates an *s* sound.

In the word "cage," the *ge* creates a *j* sound. Without that combination, there would be a hard *g* sound.

An *ing* ending creates an *ng* sound, so the *ng* needs to stay together.

Pronunciation with Diphthongs/Digraphs

Hard G	*Soft G (J sound)*
sing	singe
angle	angel
strangle	strange
courage	courageous

Like has no diphthong, so you can add *able* and drop the *e* at the end of *like* to become *likable*. With *notice*, the *ce* is a diphthong, so it becomes *noticeable*.

In some words, there are two correct answers. For example, *acknowledgment* (American spelling) and *acknowledgement (British spelling)* are both correct. More information on this topic can be found on the Internet or in any grammar book. Other sound combinations include ou, oo, oi, aw, au, ew, oy, au.

More Digraphs
ch makes the *ch* sound, as in watch, chick, chimpanzee, champion
ck makes the *k* sound, as in chick
ff makes the *f* sound, as in cliff *gh* makes the *g* sound, as in ghost, ghastly [and the *f* sound as in tough]

31

gn makes the *n* sound, as in gnome, gnarled

kn makes the *n* sound, as in knife, knight

ll makes the *l* sound, as in wall

mb makes the *m* sound, as in lamb, thumb

ng makes the *ng* sound, as in fang, boomerang, fingerprint

nk makes the *nk* sound as in ink, sink, rink

ph makes the *f* sound, as in digraph, phone, phonics

qu makes the *kw* sound, as in quick

sh makes the *sh* sound, as in shore, shipwreck, shark, shield

ss makes the *s* sound, as in floss

th makes the *th* sound, as in athlete, toothbrush, bathtub, thin, thunderstorm, this, there, that

wh makes the *hw* sound, as in where, which

wr makes the *r* sound, as in write

zz makes the *z* sound, as in fuzz and buzz

      -The above examples are from *PhonicsWorld.com*.

Exercise

Create ten words using digraphs. Discuss.

Trigraphs

chr makes the *chr* sound as in chrome, chromosome

dge makes the *ge* sound, as in dodge, partridge

tch makes the *ch* sound, as in catch, match

(From "Diphthongs," *Can Do's Helper Page*.)

Exercise

Create five words using trigraphs. Discuss.

Parallel Structure (Parallelism)

"Before You Learn" Exercise

Cover the answers below. Then correct the following sentences, to see if you make any errors.

1. Mary likes hiking, swimming, and to go bike riding.

_____

2. The production manager was asked to write his report quickly, accurately, and in a detailed manner.

_____

3. The teacher said that he was a poor student, because he waited until the last minute to study for the exam, completed his lab problems in a careless manner, and his motivation was low.

_____

4. The coach told the players that they should get a lot of sleep, not eat too much, and to do some warm-up exercises before the game.

_____

5. The salesman expected that he would present his product at the meeting, that there would be time for him to show his slide presentation, and that questions would be asked by prospective buyers.

_____

Answers
1. Mary likes hiking, swimming, and *bike riding*.
2. The production manager was asked to write his report quickly, accurately, and *thoroughly* (or completely or meticulously).
3. The teacher said that he was a poor student, because he waited until the last minute to study for the exam, completed his lab problems in a careless manner, and *he was not very motivated*.
4. The coach told the players that they should get a lot of sleep, not eat too much, and *do* some warm-up exercises before the game.
5. The sentence is correct as is.

Parallel structure confuses the most eloquent of writers, but it is simple, once you understand the rules. All the word combination in a series in the same sentence must appear in the same (parallel) format. If you begin the sentence with verbs in the present tense, you must continue in present tense, unless you have some kind of indicator (a word or phrase) that you are changing tense. If you begin using nouns, then you cannot change the list to adjectives in mid-sentence, See the examples below.

If you have verbs, all those verbs in the sentence must be in the same tense.
Verbs
A. *While my cat, Maverick, <u>looked</u> me in the eye, he <u>swallowed</u> a huge rat.*
B. *While <u>looking</u> me in the eye, my cat, Maverick, <u>swallowed</u> a huge rat.*

C. My cat, Maverick, <u>looked</u> me in the eye and <u>swallowed</u> a huge rat.

All of the above are correct. For B, it is acceptable to use both *looking* and *swallowed* because the first clause **introduces** the situation with *while*. In C, the verbs must be in the same tense because the two clauses are joined by *and*. (See "Phrases and Clauses.")

Example from a student essay:
Incorrect:
Dana realized she **wanted** to be a pediatrician, and she **can** be an inspiration to high school students who want to help others.

Wanted is past tense. Can is present tense.
This student changes tense mid-sentence, which will confuse the reader. Do the actions take place in the past or present? We do not know.

Correct:
*Dana realized she **wanted** to be a pediatrician and that she **could** be an inspiration to high school students who want to help others.*

Adjectives
If you begin with adjectives in your sentence, then you must stay with adjectives and not change them to verb/adjective/noun combinations as in the example below.
They must all be in the same format when they appear as a series in the same sentence.

Incorrect:
She was neat, clean, and had a friendly demeanor.

Correct:
She was neat, clean, and friendly.

Nouns
The same rule applies to nouns. You must keep your nouns parallel in order to be clear and concise.

Example from a student essay.

Incorrect:
The disease caused Jacob several side effects, such as constant seizures, not being able to walk straight, and harder to grasp objects.

In the above example, once the student begins with a noun, she should continue using nouns, or begin a new sentence.

Correct:
The disease caused Jacob several side effects, such as constant seizures, a crooked walk, and difficulty grasping objects.

The nouns *seizures, walk,* and *difficulty* can be used with or without adjectives. If you use an adjective for one, you are not obligated to do the same for all of the nouns in the sentence.

Phrases
Phrases are longer groups of words, so you must think of each phrase and match it to the other phrases in the sentence. Most phrases are set apart by commas, which can help you and the reader to absorb the ideas in them, before moving through the rest of the sentence.

Incorrect:
She walked to the store, bought ice cream, and <u>was talking</u> to Bob.

Correct:
She walked to the store, bought ice cream, and <u>talked</u> to Bob.
Since the writer begins in the past tense, all the verbs must remain in the past tense.

Use parallel structure when using connecting words, such as *for, and, nor, but,* or words that work in pairs, such as *not only, but also; either/or; neither/nor,* etc.

She neither wants a new car nor a new hat.

She is, not only very sweet but also punctual and capable.
There is no need to repeat the verb *is* for the adjectives *punctual* and *capable*.

Also acceptable:
Not only is she very sweet, but she is also punctual and capable.

Exercise
First, cover the answers below.

1. Students either study, or they will fail.
2. Scientists study, research, and they do a lot of experimenting to formulate their theories.
3. She was fit, pretty, and looked young.
4. Children need not only discipline but also to have fun.
5. Many of us like neither carrots nor to eat broccoli.
6. She cannot dance in dance class, study her math, and then also be partying all night.

Answers
1. Students either study *or fail.*
2. Scientists study, research, and *experiment a lot* to formulate their theories. (See "Odd Word Usages.")
3. She was fit, pretty, and *youthful* (or *young-looking*).

4. Children need not only discipline *but also fun*.
5. Many of us like neither carrots *nor broccoli*.
6. She cannot dance in dance class, study her math, and then also party all night.

Polite/Formal Language

When we meet someone who uses very respectful and formal English, we tend to respect that person. Proper language influences those who listen to us. It is especially useful in formal writing. Oftentimes, it is preferable to replace informal with formal speech.

Examples:
Say "very well" instead of "okay" or "all right."
Avoid contractions. Say "cannot" instead of "can't."
Say "good day," instead of "hi."

Avoid saying "you" unless speaking directly to the reader, as I do in this book. Saying "you" gives the book a personal tone. This is considered informal writing.

Informal: *When you get on the bus, have your money ready in advance.*
Formal: *Before someone gets on the bus, he should have his money ready in advance.*

Informal: *Can you ...?*
Formal: *Would you mind ...?*

Informal: *Sorry ...*
Formal: *I apologize ... or I am terribly sorry.*

Informal: *Can you open the door for me?*
Formal: *Will you kindly open the door for me?*

Exercise
Using the examples listed above, write three formal and informal sentences. Discuss.

For more on using formal English, go to http://polite-english.com/.

Odd Word Usages, Errors in Logic, and Jokes

This chapter includes examples of odd word usage as well as correct and incorrect logic. As you go through your day, see if you can distinguish among them.

Odd word usages
A lot. This can mean a parking lot or a piece of ground. It also is used to mean a great deal or a great many.

Thanks God. The correct expression is, *Thank God*, as in, "Thank you, God," or "I thank God." "Thanks, God" is also acceptable if you are thanking God directly. In that case, a comma is needed.

Out of respect, people often (but not always) capitalize the pronouns that refer to God. Pagan gods, for example, the Greek gods, usually are not capitalized. This rule can be applied even if you do not believe in God; you are showing respect in spite of what you personally feel.

Irregardless. There is no such word. Say "regardless," which means without regard. Adding *ir* makes the meaning "without regard without." Two minuses make a plus. This is a double negative in one word. Double negatives are not permitted in English. It is like saying "I do not have none," which means "I have some." However, it is acceptable to say "irrespective" and "irresponsible."

Mary felt in love. It should be *Mary fell in love*.

I appreciated. The writer means to say, *I appreciate it*.

"I had a blast at the summit … I attended some classes and learned a magnanimous amount of information …"
—Ismael M., writer from writer and executive testimonials from the 2011 Pitch Summit (pitching meeting for writers) found in an Ink Tip (writers' online magazine) email, May 5, 2011:
Magnanimous means generous in a big way in being forgiving and courageous, as in "He is a magnanimous person."

"… on that faithful day …"
The correct phrase is *fateful day*, a reference to destiny.

"Claritin: The first and only *non-drowsy medicine*."
—TV commercial
Medicines do not get drowsy. People do.

"It is very *worrying*."
This should say *worrisome*. It makes us worry. The word *worrying* in this context is becoming increasingly popular, and therefore can be considered correct, but I always stay with the old, tried and true manner of speech.

"She would not be able to *bare* his children" (i.e., undress his children).
"We have the right to *bare* arms" (i.e., have naked arms).
Bare means to make be naked. *Bear* (meaning "to carry") should have been used in both cases.

"When I heard about those great insurance rates, I *literally* fell out of my chair."
—Car insurance TV commercial
Using "literally" means she really did fall.

"Children with a disability …"
—student essay
The above error is very common. She means, "Children with *disabilities*." If you say, "Children with a disability …," then you mean that they all share one disability. Keep both in the plural or in the singular, for example, "a child with a disability," unless the child has more than one disability. In that case, you would say, "A child with multiple disabilities …"

"In this book, *A Thousand Small Sparrows* …."
This book? Is it right here? Say "in the book" or "in his book, *A Thousand Small Sparrows*, Jeff Leeland …"

Errors in Logic
"I have been following you since 1998, and you never fail to disappoint. Loved, loved, loved the Webinar BootCamp!"
– A comment from Marcie, the Empress of Sales. Found in Jeffrey Gitomer's *Sales Caffeine* #529 ~ "What's WRONG With These Kids?" online magazine.

"Find out what can you do."
This mixes a statement with a question. It should be:
Find out what you can do.

"I'm not jealous of anyone here, and that's on my mother's life, God strike her dead."
—Taylor on VH1's *Tough Love*
What is wrong with this statement?

"I can't imagine what I'd do if my child showed up missing."
—*Law and Order: SVU*
If she "showed up," then she would not be missing.

"He neglected his duties as governor to protect his people."
— *The Empress* by Anchee Min
There is a logic problem here. His duty *is* to protect. Does the author mean that he neglected his duties as governor *in order to protect* his people or that he neglected his duties as governor, *which were to protect* his people?

"Having money means freed from want, beauty, luxury …"
—Napoleon Hill, *How to Be Rich*
Although Hill was very wise and gave great advice, his language skills left something to be desired. The correct way to have said this is, "Having money means being free from want and having beauty, luxury …" Otherwise, it reads like the person wants to be freed from beauty and luxury as well.

"Although often unpleasant, life comes along with bitter obstacles."
—Student essay
When "although" is used, the next clause must take the opposite attitude from the previous clause. Since the student begins with a negative, she must end with a positive.

If she wants to keep both clauses negative, she could have said: "Because it is often unpleasant, life comes along with bitter obstacles." However, I would not say "life comes along." Life is already here. She could say, "life gives us." This is one reason why rewriting is so very important.

Jokes:
"Varicose brains."
—Stephen Colbert, *The Colbert Report.*
This is an intentional witticism that references "varicose veins," meaning that the brains are decaying.

"The alternatives can be fetal."
Another joke; this is a pun on "fatal."

"Are you Tom Semenko, the genius? That's redundant."
—Diane on *Cheers*
Intentionally witty. Can you tell why?

"I liked Pluto, ergo, I don't like you."
—Sheldon on *The Big Bang Theory*
The man to whom Sheldon is speaking is the one who demoted Pluto from planet to something less impressive, and Sheldon is angry about that. This is an intelligent, yet childish sentence, which reflects his character—socially awkward and brilliant.

Exercise
Rewrite the following sentences correctly. Discuss.

1. He ain't got no sense.
2. There's a stigmatism to ageing.
3. He follows his conscious.
4. "It's a guttural instinct." – Carson Daly with MichelleMonachan, actor.
5. "Ghost Busters. Who you gonna call?"
6. He gave me an idea that I loved it.

Answers
1. He has no sense. He doesn't have any sense.
2. stigma. *Stigmatism* is a problem with eyesight.
3. conscience. *Conscious* means awake and aware.

4. gut instinct means from one's gut or instinct. *Gutteral* mean a low voice which comes from deep down.

5. Whom are you going to call?

6**.** He gave me an idea that I loved. or He gave me an idea, and I loved it.

Racist or Sexist Language

Racist Language

Racist language is any word or phrase that denigrates or belittles an individual or group by referring to his or her race. It is usually based on fear, ignorance, and stereoptypes and is rooted in the "us versus them," way of thinking.

The "N" word: Notice that I do not even write the word for which the *N* stands. In the 1950s, polite people used the word "colored" to indicate anyone who was not white. "Negro" was used specifically to describe black people. In the 1960s, the Black Panthers coined the phrase "Black Power." Now we use the words "black" and African American, and other outdated words have fallen by the wayside. Using the *N* word in literature usually shows how wrong it is, or it merely serves as a tool to reveal character and is not usually meant, by the author, to be racist. See the novel, *To Kill a Mockingbird*, by Harper Lee for an example of this.

Here is a list of a few other improper words.

Gypped means being cheated; it refers to gypsies, who have been stereotyped as thieves. "He gypped me" is a racist comment. In the same way, *jewed* is derogatory to Jewish people.

Indian Summer, Indian Giver. These mean false summer and one who takes back what he gave.

Philistine: Once I asked a student, "How do you say *Palestinian* in Arabic?" She said, "Philistine." I was shocked, but a light bulb went on in my head. There has been so much racism directed against the Palestinians, even today. In the Bible, they are the bad people. Goliath, who was slain by David, was Philistine.. The dictionary says Philistines are people who lack cultural values. They are also people from ancient Philistia, which is southwest Palestine

    -See Dictionary.com.

Philistine(s), Palestine, Philistia: The Philistines are descendants of the Casluhim, who were sons of Mizraim, son of Ham, son of Noah (Genesis 10:14)

This name seems to be related to the verb (*palash* 1779), which indicates a rather hysterical action, induced by grief and involving dust or ashes to roll around in (Micah 1:10). BDB Theological Dictionary hints at similar verbs in cognate languages, which reveal the more fundamental meaning of burrow into, break into. As a nation, the Philistines seem to have been known as the Steamrollers.

Archaeologists have proven the Philistines to have come from Greece, immigrated into Egypt and then, like the Hebrews, moved to a land they called Palestine. Remnants of a Hebrew occupation of Goshen are not found, and neither proof of the Hebrew wandering years. During the reign of David the Philistines and their culture ceased to be in the land of Israel."
-From Dictionary.com

"The sign of a Philistine age is the cry of immorality against art."
—Oscar Wilde

"Our society distributes itself into Barbarians, Philistines and Populace; and America is just ourselves with the Barbarians quite left out, and the Populace nearly."
—Matthew Arnold
-From *Dictionary.com*.

Hispanic. Many of my students and colleagues of Mexican and Latin American descent do not like to be called Hispanic; they prefer Latino.

Caucasian. I do not like to be called *Caucasian* or *Gentile*. My people are not from the Caucasus **region of the world**. Call me either white or English/German.
In some translations of scripture, *gentile* means heathen or nonbeliever, but the connotation of *heathen* is one who is uncivilized.

Exercise
Discuss how we can avoid using racist words or phrases.

Sexist Language
Sexist language is any word or phrase that denigrates or belittles by referring to someone's gender. Below is an example of sexism during a presidential race. People seem more afraid to express racist feelings than they do sexist attitudes.

So, some criticism is valid, some is sexist in nature, and it's extremely disappointing that the press isn't talking about it at all. I was stunned when a McCain supporter called Hillary Clinton a "bitch," and McCain actually used it as a fundraising tool. The media shrugged it off. Then, last week, Chris Rock, upon introducing Obama, jokingly warned African Americans not to support "that white lady," which oddly has only been reported as a story about race, not gender.

There's a gender issue here, in both cases, that is not being addressed …

Here are just a few examples of what out there.: One is, "Hillary Clinton: Stop Running for President and Make Me a Sandwich." So this is out there , and it is not really being discussed. I'm not sure if that's helpful or harmful to Hillary Clinton. I just know it disgusts me.
-Bkgrl. *My Direct Democracy*, "Hillary Clinton Facing Undiscussed Sexism"

Discuss how people can avoid using sexist words or phrases. What are situations in which sexist or racist language has been used? Should any specific groups allowed to use such words or phrases?

Redundancies

Being redundant is when we say the same thing in two different ways. In other words, we repeat ourselves. Avoid this. Sometimes, we purposely repeat a thought or phrase for emphasis. Below are unintended redundancies, and they weaken the writers' statements.

In my opinion, I think ...
If you think it, then it is your opinion.

"After Stephanie was introduced to the high school students, people just wanted to help. 'Everyone wanted to volunteer' (Leeland 145)."—student essay
To avoid being redundant, say:
"After Stephanie was introduced to the high school students, 'Everyone wanted to volunteer' (Leeland 145)."

The above run-on sentence is how Leeland wrote it.

Exercise
Write three redundancies in sentences, and then three sentences with the redundancies corrected. Discuss.

Commonly Misused Words

The below list gives you an idea of just a few words that many of us misuse.

Healthy versus Healthful
It is not a healthy breakfast if there is dead material in the bowl. It is *healthful*, because it fills us with health.

Correct: She is a *healthy* child.
Correct: He has a *healthy* attitude. An attitude is a state of being and can be ill or well.

Incorrect: She lives a healthy lifestyle.
Correct: She lives a *healthful* lifestyle

Hard versus Difficult
Hard is a physical surface or a metaphor.

Incorrect: It is a hard situation.
Correct: It is a *difficult* situation.

It is a *hard* chair or surface.
He is a very *hard* (i.e., cruel, strict, tough, or coarse) man.
Life hit her with many *hard* knocks.
Life is *difficult*.

Quotation versus Quote
Quotation is a noun; *to quote* is an infinitive verb.

Few versus Little
This road has very *little* trees (The trees are small.).
This road has very *few* trees (There are not many trees along this road.).

Advertising versus advertisement
Advertising is the general idea of getting the message out.
An *advertisement* is a specific poster, announcement, or commercial; it is abbreviated as *ad*.

Bunch of
There were a bunch of people. I have a bunch of time.
These sentences are incorrect, because a bunch is a group of attached fruit or anything else, as in a *bunch* of grapes.

Logic

In its simplest form, logic is when we use reason to follow a train of thought and come up with a plausible conclusion based on the evidence we have. Sometimes we say illogical things, Below are some of them.

"Are you a pathological liar?"–
—CNN reporter Paula Zahn interviewing Stephen Glass, who falsified several magazine stories. Why would she expect a truthful answer from a liar? She may feel obligated to ask this, since her viewers may want to ask that question.

"This is my story, and I'm gonna put meaning to these words."
—A rapper on TV
The rapper is assuming that the words themselves have no meaning.

A parent says, *"Do you want me to take away your IPad?"* knowing that the child does not. This is a veiled threat which means, "I will take away your IPad if you do not do as I wish." It may not be a logical question, but parents feel that it is effective.

Exercise
Write three illogical sentences, and then rewrite the three sentences to make them logical. Discuss.

Word Roots

Many words are made up of a root (or base word) and a prefix. They often have suffixes attached as well. The root is the main part of the word. The prefix is attached to the beginning of the word root as in precede. *Cede*(meaning arrive) is the root and *pre* (meaning before) is the prefix of the first word in the below list.

morph= shape
Anthropormorphic, metamorphosis, morphology

pre = before   cede= arrive
precede = arriving before
prepaid = paid before
prevent = act before
predict = say before

milli = thousand pede=foot
millipede = arthropod with a thousand feet
millimeter= measure of a thousand

pedesone who goes on foot
pedestrian= travelling on foot

Exercise
Using a dictionary or your memory, find ten word roots, and combine them into words.

Prefixes and Suffixes

Meanings are attached to the beginnings and endings of roots.

Prefixes
A prefix is attached to the root at the beginning of a word, and the suffix is attached to the root at the end of the word.

Pre = before, fix = attached

ab or a= from, away, apart
abnormal, abrupt, aberration

bene,ben=good
beneficial,beneficent

Suffixes
Suf = after, fix = attached

Lith= stone
Monolith,lithograph, megalith

ing= expresses the ongoing action of the verb to which it is attached.
Ex: digging

ly-=Having the qualities of, occurring at certain intervals. Ly often turns an adjective into an adverb.

Example: The adjective *kind* becomes the adverb *kindly*. He is *kind*. He *kindly* gave up his seat for me.

Misused Prefixes and Suffixes

Not uncredible, but *incredible*. *In* is the prefix and *ible* is the suffix attached to *cred*, which means *believe*.

Not machure, but *mature*. From Latin *maturare* meaning *to ripen*. *Chure* is not a suffix

Not inderstand, but *understand,* which means *to comprehend.*
Under is the *prefix. Stand* is the root.

Exercise

Combine any of the below suffixes, prefixes, and word roots to create words. Write five sentences using the words you created. Discuss.

len	tify
cap	bid
quan	ient
sen	tity
mor	ible
love	able
a	mobile
im	bility

Exercise

Using a dictionary or your memory, find five prefixes and five suffixes, and combine them into words. Write sentences using those words.

Spelling and Pronunciation

Exercise
Cover the answers below. Then circle the correct spelling of the words below:

1. (a) receive   (b) receive
2. (a) commited   (b) committed
3. (a) meaness   (b) meanness
4. (a) likeable   (b) likable
5. (a) base ball   (b) baseball

Answers
1. a
2. b
3. b
4. b
5. b

There are basic rules to spelling.

Spelling with the letters *ie and ei*

Words that have either *ie* or *ei* have specific rules.
The saying goes, "I before e, except after c, or when sounded as "a," as in neighbor and weigh."

I before *e*: *friend, believe.*
Except after *c*: *receipt, ceiling.*
When sounded as *a*: *neigh, reign, feign*

There are some exceptions, including *weird, ancient, leisure, their, forfeit, foreign.*

Double the Final Consonant
If a word has a vowel before a final consonant, as in *commit*, double the consonant before adding the ending: *commit/committed shop/shopped, hop/hopped, permit/permitted. Shop/shopping, hop/hopping, permit/permitting.*

If a word has a double vowel before the final consonant, leave that consonant alone: *scoop/ scooped, clean/cleaner.*

If a word has an *e* at the end, add "d" to make it past tense: *dine/ dined, hope/ hoped. Dine/dining, hope/hoping. Dine/diner not dinner which is the day's last meal.*

Words Spelled the Same but Accentuated Differently
to con*sole* (comfort), a *con*sole (grouping)

to re*cord* (make a record of), a *rec*ord (the record itself),
*in*valid (ill person), in*val*id (not correct).

Words People often Pronounce Incorrectly

Some say *nucular* when they mean *nuclear*. There is no such word as nucular. This is a mispronunciation. Some people in some parts of the US speak like this. There are many articles written on this since George W. Bush said this word during his presidency.
Some say, "He and I have a good *repore*," when they mean *rapport* (sounds like "rap-ore").

Some say, "That is a *pitcher* of me when I was ten," when they should say *picture* (sounds like "pik-chure").

These glaring pronunciation errors make us seem less than bright, so please learn to speak them properly.

Vocabulary

We need to know many words to successfully operate in society. Below is a short quiz to see how well you know some of them.

Exercise

Cover the answers below. Then circle (a) or (b) to indicate the correct meaning of a word.

1. adapt   (a) acclimatize   (b) resist
2. adept   (a) adapt   (b) good at
3. statute   (a) statue   (b) law
4. console   (a) comfort   (b) counsel
5. desert   (a) sweet food   (b) dry landscape
6. allegiance   (a) prominence   (b) loyalty
7. advise   (a) to give an opinion (b) the opinion itself

Answers

1. a
2. b
3. b
4. a
5. b
6. b
7. a

Now, create your own list, and test your classmates. Use your dictionary or thesaurus.

Work to build your vocabulary. Reading helps us to do that. When I hear or read a new word, I make it a point to remember it and use it. Words are powerful. Just the right word can make all the difference.

Common Errors in Wording/Syntax

The below are errors I have taken directly from student essays over the years. Syntax is the way sentences are worded, as in word order or phraseology. Many of these sentences have syntax or logic problems.

In Marcielle Brandler's poem, "When I Used to Drive the Fast Lane" (*The Breathing House*, iUniverse), tells a story about a longing for love and how easy it is to get distracted on the …"

The writer states "In Marcielle's poem … tells." The words in-between are an interruption that can distract the writer from creating a complete sentence.

Two better options:
In Marcielle Brandler's poem, "When I Used to Drive the Fast Lane" (*The Breathing House*, iUniverse), she tells …

Marcielle Brandler's poem, "When I Used to Drive the Fast Lane" (*The Breathing House*, iUniverse), tells …

Can you see the small but important difference?

I had to rewrite a sentence in this very book. See below:

My website includes a review of a Kevin Kline film that I wrote.
Word order here can lead the reader to believe that I wrote the film, so I reworded it to say:
My website includes a review that I wrote of a Kevin Kline film.

Can you see the difference?

I *want to aspire* to be a great writer.
The writer wants to want.

She was an African-American *mixed* with white student.
Does this mean she is one African-American among many whites, or is she mixed blood?

In *my opinion, I think* that we should have gay marriage.
The writer is saying, "I think, I think," which is a redundancy.

E-mail invitation for a Law-of-Attraction event:
    Ready to get out of this stressed induced economic crisis and experience REAL

ENLIGHTENMENT?

Ever wonder WHY is this happening to me AGAIN?

Want to learn the MOST POWERFUL SECRET in Forgiveness and its connection to Abundance?

Are you READY to STOP THE INSANITY of your LIFE and Starting Living Prosperously?

Can you identify the numerous errors in the above ad? Why do you think the creators of the ad worded it this way?

Signs at Businesses

Restaurant: *scramble eggs* This should me *scrambled eggs.*

Flower shop: *long stem roses.* This should be *long-stemmed roses.*

Police station, in a cordoned-off area: *Caution: Bee's*

In this last example, bees should be plural, *Bees* (not possessive). But a student could say, "I got five *B's* in English class."

Other Examples:

"Hi professor Brandler, I just wanted to let you know that I am not going to be able to attend class on Monday, July 6. I'm really sorry. I would appreciated if you could let me know if there is anything i should be working on for tuesday. Thanks for your comprehension, I'll be seeing you on tuesday, have a nice day."

—Note from a student

There are several errors here. Can you identify them? "The U.S. government has just served up a mouthful to people who eat."

—Melissa Healy, This seems to suggest that some people do not eat.

"This is a 'relationship business' ... and their is no better way to create professional business relationships with others in the Entertainment Industry than through the power of networking!"

—Show Biz Expo e-mail

Where is the error? How does this writer appear in the eyes of a reader?

"I have two children who have fetal alcohol syndrome. Alcohol is worse than marijuana."

—Radio show caller, *The Pat Morrison Show*, KPCC Radio, November 3 2010.

It does not follow that one condition is worse than another merely because a person says so. Where is her reasoning? This is not logical.

"If you or a loved one took Avandia and suffered heart attack, stroke, or death, call this number." —TV ad

How can a dead person call anyone? The writer is trying to say several things in one sentence and hopes that viewers will get it, logical or not.

Exercise
Choose five of the above incorrect sentences, and rewrite them correctly. Discuss.

Typical English as a Second Language (ESL) Mistakes

Many people whose first language is not English, use constructions from their first language when they speak English. That can cause problems with meanings and sometimes the listener or reader will not be able to figure out what we mean. Below are just a few such examples.

Those cats are mines.
This is a common mistake among Spanish speakers, because Spanish pronouns are plural when objects are plural. Because *cats* is plural, so is *mine*. They say in Spanish, *Los gatos son mios.* However, English speakers say *Those cats are mine.* If non-native speakers compare their mistakes in English to practices within their own languages, they will find it easier to learn English.

She didn't went with me.
This is a logical mistake made by many Arabic speakers. It is logical because *didn't* is past tense, so the speaker assumes that *went* (the past tense of *go*) is right. The correct sentence is "she didn't go with me."

She is depress.
The above error comes from hearing the language and not seeing it written. If one listens more carefully, one can hear the *t* sound at the end of the word. The correct sentence is "She is depressed."

Adjectives and Adverbs

Adjectives
Adjectives modify (describe or give information about) nouns.

A girl. What kind of girl? A _____ girl or a girl who is _____. The blank space represents where we would place the adjective.
beautiful
tall
slender
stately
kind
sad

These are all words that tell more about girl.

Currently the words *the, a,* and *an* also describe nouns and act as adjectives. Many of us were taught that these were only articles. In "that is a *blue* car," blue describes the car. Grammar books now call *the, a,* and *an* adjectives because they explain *which* car.

Exercise
Cover the answers below, and then circle the adjectives in these sentences:
1. Skunks smell (bad/badly).
2. I don't feel (good/well).
3. My friend, Sesshu was (real/really) tall.
4. That is very (good/well) writing.
5. He writes very (good/well).

Answers
1. They smell *bad.* They are not *doing* anything. They are *being.* See "Linking Verbs" for more information.
2. I don't feel *well.*
3. My friend Sesshu was *really* tall. This is not a very good word to use, but it is common. *Very* would be better.
4. That is very *good* writing.
5. He writes very *well.*

Do it again. Cover the answers, and circle the adjective in the sentences below.
1. He ran so (fast/quickly) I couldn't keep up with him.
2. He is not a (good/well) person.
3. Do I dare to drive (fast/rapidly) in all this traffic?
4. He likes (fast/fastly) women and cars.
5. She laughs (loud/loudly).
6. She is (loud/loudly).

Answers
1. He ran so *quickly* (adverb) I couldn't keep up with him.
2. He is not a *good* (adjective) person, and he is not a *well* person are both correct. It depends on what is meant. Use *good* to indicate morality. Use *well* to indicate mental or physical health.
3. Do I dare to drive *rapidly* (adjective) in all this traffic? Yes, fast sounds correct, but that is because we all use it so often. Because the word fast is short and is spoken quickly, we like to use it. It sounds like what it means (onomatopoeia).
4. He likes *fast* (adjective) women and cars. There is no such word as fastly.
5. She laughs *loudly.* (adverb)
6. She is *loud.* (adjective)

Comparative/Superlative Adjectives
We compare two things. For example, "Bob is taller than Mary," or "Bob is the taller of the two." We would never say "Bob is more taller."

A superlative is the maximum of the noun being described. The difficult part is saying the phrase correctly..
We would not say, "She is the most brightest girl."
The chart below will help.

Adjective	Comparative	Superlative
bright	brighter	brightest
good	better	best
small	smaller	smallest
big	bigger	biggest
beautiful	more beautiful	most beautiful
organized	more organized	most organized
organized	less organized	least organized

There are several differences between the adjectives listed above.

One-syllable adjectives:
If an adjective is made of one syllable, then add *er* or *est* to the end. If it ends with one consonant preceded by a vowel, double the consonant and add the correct ending. See *big* in the chart above.

Two-syllable adjectives:
Use *more* and *most* with most two-syllable adjectives, except those ending in *y*. See the above chart.

Two-syllable adjectives ending in *y*:
Change the *y* to *i*, and add *er* for the comparative and *est* for the superlative. For example, happy, happier, and happiest; hungry, hungrier, and hungriest. For more information, check out the websites in the "Works Cited" section of this book.

Three-syllable adjectives:
Usually, you must use more and most with words that have three syllables.
Ex: *fantastic, colorful, bountiful, courageous, limited, complicated, eccentric, devious.*

Exercise
Make comparatives and superlatives using the words below.
1. dominant
2. silly
3. secretive
4. heavenly
5. conscious

Answers
1. more dominant, most dominant. *Dominant* has three syllables. See the rules.
2. sillier, silliest

3. more secretive, most secretive
4. more heavenly, most heavenly Remember that *heavenly* has three syllables.
5. more conscious, most conscious

Hyphenated Modifiers
Some word combinations act as adjectives. The punctuation may change when word combinations are used to modify a noun.

Examples:
My car needs a fuel that has high octane.
My car uses *high-octane* fuel (hyphenated modifier).

I see him every day.
I see him on an *everyday* basis (hyphenated modifier).

There is no need to add a hyphen to everyday in this case. When used as a modifier, *everyday* is not hyphenated. It may be that is was used this way so frequently, society just began to accept it. Remember that language changes.

an out-of-shape friend
well-groomed fields
well-to-do folks
black-and-white television
behind-the-scenes power broker

Exercise
Create sentences using these phrases as modifiers.
1. step by step
2. high speed
3. over the top
4. long term
5. in the style of the Spanish
6. well known
7. well spoken.

Adverbs
Adverbs have three jobs. They modify verbs, adjectives, and other adverbs.

Verbs:
She is walking. How is she is walking?
slowly
sluggishly
quickly
(*Fast* is an adjective. Do not use it here.)

Adjectives:
That girl is beautiful. How beautiful?
very
extremely
somewhat
dazzlingly
dangerously

Notice that these words are qualifiers. They tell how much.

Adverbs:
Use the same words used to modify an adjective.
She is walking *sluggishly*. How sluggishly is she walking?
very
extremely
somewhat
dazzlingly
dangerously

These qualifiers are overused words and should be avoided if possible. Instead of saying she walks *terribly sluggishly*, just say *sluggishly*. That word tells us all we need to know. Adding more words just slows down the sentence and detracts from the power of *sluggishly*: although, because it slows down the sentence with an extra word, it makes it more sluggish. Thus, you must use your own judgment in these matters.

Exercise
Cover the answers below. Then, circle the correct adverb.
1. He dances (superb/superbly).
2. I thought she played the violin (good/well).
3. Sometimes, our lives do not run as (smooth/smoothly) as we would like.
4. He is (very/kind of) awkward.

Answers
1. He dances *superbly*.
2. I thought she played the violin *well*. Remember, we are good, and we *do* well.
3. Sometimes, our lives do not run as *smoothly* as we would like.
4. He is *very* awkward. Kind of is not a correct phrase, although people do use it in speech. Avoid it in writing. Awkward is an adjective, so its modifier (very) is an adverb.

Now change these sentences to make adjectives. Cover the answers below, and circle the correct answers.
1. He is (superb/superbly).
2. I thought she looked (good/well).
3. Sometimes, our lives are not as (smooth/smoothly) as we would like.
4. He is (awkward/awkwardly).

Answers
1. He is *superb*.
2. I thought she looked *well* (if you are referring to health), and I thought she looked *good* (if you are referring to appearance).
3. Sometimes, our lives are not as *smooth* as we would like.
4. He is *awkward*.

Number, Amount, and Count and Non-count Nouns

Many people get mixed up with count and non-count nouns and how to use them. There are specific rules that govern this.

The amount of apps is never-ending.
—Cell phone commercial.

Amount is used something in a mass, like a bowl of sugar, such as "the amount of sugar." But use *number* for apps (applications) because they can be counted. Anything that can be counted should be a number.

Example:
There are a *number* of people here.
There is a great *amount* of water in the ocean.
You cannot count how many water molecules there are in the ocean. It is a mass, so it is non-count noun.

With *fewer* and *less*, the same rule applies. Fewer is for something we can count, and less is for a mass. For example, *fewer* people; *less* sugar.

Exercise
Cover the answers. Identify the count (number of) nouns with a *C* and non-count (mass) nouns with an *N*. Include *Ab* for abstract nouns and *Con* for concrete nouns.

1. __ hospital
2. __ decision
3. __ lecture
4. __ dirt
5. __ mashed potatoes
6. __ key
7. __ hair
8. __ hairs
9. __ potatoes
10. __ a bowl of sugar
11. __ sugar cubes

Answers
1. C/Con
2. C/Ab. Even though this is a abstract noun, it still can be counted.
3. C/Ab. If we were referring to the written lecture, it would be a concrete noun.
4. N/Con
5. N/Con
6. C/con
7. N/Con
8. C/Con
9. C/Con
10. N/Con
11. C/Con

Collective Nouns
Some nouns have a plural understanding in the words themselves. There is more than one of whatever it is, which is understood in the singular of the noun.

Audience is a group of people. It is one audience but it means that there is a group of people watching a performance. *Bunch* is a group of fruit stuck together like grapes. (Never say "a bunch of people." That sounds very childlike. Say *many people* or *several people*, instead.)

Exercise
Cover the answers. Put a C next to the collective nouns. Leave the others blank.

1. __ apple
2. __ horses
3. __ herd
4. __ gaggle (of geese)
5. __ mission
6. __ crew
7. __ faculty
8. __ platoon

Answers
1. _
2. _
3. C
4. C
5. _
6. C
7. C
8. C

Conjunctions

Conjunctions are words that join.
Con = with
Junction = join.
We join sentences, phrases, nouns, and verbs with conjunctions.

Phrase
As she hobbled along, he walked protectively behind her.
The *as* in "as she hobbled along," acts as a conjunction. It is understood that there will just be a comma before the next clause. Another way to write this sentence: He walked protectively behind her, as she hobbled along. Now, it is easy to identify the conjunction.

Sentence
I was walking with Bob, when I saw the cutest cat.
We have joined two sentences with "when."

Nouns
Mary and Bill will be here.
We have united Mary and Bill using "and."

Here is a partial list of conjunctions: but, and, yet, as after, although, since, until, unless, as, as if, because, when, where, whenever, while, neither, either, neither/nor, either/or, not only but also.

Exercise
Write five sentences using the conjunctions listed above. Discuss.

Beginning Sentences with Conjunctions
"But you said I could." We see this kind of incorrect construction all the time in books and magazines, and we hear it in speech. According to the *Chicago Manual of Style*, it is acceptable to begin a sentence with a conjunction, but many educators consider it incorrect. Conjunctions join sentences, nouns, and phrases to each other inside sentences.

Examples of correct conjunction usage:
Mary *and* Bob are here.
I climbed the hill *but* could not see the valley below.
He his wealthy, *yet* he dresses like an average person.

Phrases and Clauses

Prepositional Phrases
Prepositional phrases begin with a preposition and link the *subject* to its *object*. If there is a preposition, an object will follow, unless the preposition is being used for some other purpose, such as in the phrase, *to walk,* which is an infinitive phrase. *English the Easy Way*, a workbook, has a nice list of prepositional phrases. List of prepositions are also available online.

Examples of Prepositions:
on, under, underneath, through, throughout, in, inside, over, above, except, since, between, during, against, until, past, around

Abstract (nonphysical) prepositions, like *except, during*, and *since*, can be the most difficult to spot, because we cannot experience them in the physical world. We cannot see or touch them.

Exercise
Cover the answers below. Then circle the prepositions, and underline the prepositional phrases.

1. Through the house ran the mouse to its nest.
2. I cannot see inside that dark corner with its scary atmosphere.
3. Although Ezekiel is a very respectable young man, Candace's parents will not allow her to go with him.

Answers
1. (*Through* the house) … (*to* its nest)
2. (*inside* that dark corner) … (*with* its scary atmosphere)
3. (*with* her)

Write five sentences using prepositional phrases. Circle the preposition, and underline the prepositional phrase. Discuss.

The Object of the Preposition

When a noun or pronoun occurs after a preposition, it will be in the objective case. Examine the Subject/Object chart, then continue.

Exercise
Cover the answers below.

1. May I borrow the frying pan from you and (she/her)?

2. The music began with Madeline and (I/me), as we sang our new song.
3. Among the singers and (I/me), there was a fabulous baritone.

Answers
1. May I borrow the frying pan from you and her.
2. The music began with Madeline and me … (Remember that the music began *with me*. Forget Madeline for now.)
3. Among the singers and me, there was a fabulous baritone.
If the preposition *among* makes it too difficult to figure out the object, use *with*. You would say, "with me," not "with I."

You would never say *Bob* (subject) said hello to *I* (another subject). You would say *Bob* said hello to *me* (object). The same goes when more than one person serve as the object.

Exercise
Now that you understand, try three more, and I bet that you will do better. First, cover the answers below.

1. My friends signaled to James and (I/me) to pull the car over.
2. The concert was paid for by the production company and (he/him).
3. Everyone, except Bob and (we/us), was at the party.

Answers
1. My friends signaled to James and *me* to pull the car over.
2. The concert was paid for by the production company and him
3. Everyone, except Bob and *us*, was at the party

Infinitive Phrases (Verbs)

To walk is an infinitive phrase, because it is not conjugated. It is not in the present, past, or future tenses. It is not limited to one time frame; therefore, it is called infinitive.

Spanish infinitives are usually one word, while English infinitives are two words.

English	Spanish
to walk	caminar
to laugh	reír
to see	ver

Try not to separate the two words in an infinitive. Do not say, for example, *to never walk*. This is called a *split infinitive*. Say *never to walk*.
Infinitives are not conjugated. They have no past, present, or future. They merely are.

The Chicago Manual of Style says that it is sometime permitted to split infinitives as in, "They expect *to* more than *double* their income next year." *To double* is the verb.

59

Infinitives usually act as nouns.

I love *to walk*. I love *walking*. Love is the verb. *To walk* and *walking* are the objects that are loved. They are nouns.

Exercise

Cover the answers below. Then, underline the infinitive phrase.

1. Can Jill learn to dance with that prosthetic leg?
2. Many believe that General George Armstrong Custer forced his men to fight and to die for the sake of his ego.

Answers

1. to dance
2. to fight, to die

Now, write five sentences using infinitive phrases.

Clauses

Independent Clauses

Independent clauses are complete sentences. All that is need are a subject and verb. For example, you ask, "What did Mary do all day?" Your friend answers, "She slept." *She slept* is a complete sentence, because it has a *subject* doing or being the *verb*.

Dependent Clauses

A dependent clause is an incomplete sentence or a "fragment." We can say, "She slept," but if we begin that sentence with *although*, it changes it to an incomplete thought: "Although she slept ..." We need more information. What happened while she slept?

When speaking, we often use incomplete sentences. We speak in code and shortened thoughts. The other person is there to ask, nod, or squint for clarification. There are visual and sound cues that prompt us to complete our communication. That is not the case with formal or any other kind of writing. Write completely and clearly to avoid any possible misinterpretation.

You can place fragments at the beginning or the end of a sentence.

If you go with me, I will pay your way.
I will pay your way, if you go with me.

The independent clause, *I will pay your way*, is a complete sentence and can stand alone. But *if you go with me* must be attached to a complete sentence to have meaning. It is *dependent* upon the independent clause.

Independent clauses can be interrupted by dependent clauses, which usually act as adjectives and describe the subject.
Example:
Bob, who is my best friend, *will be here.*
Bob will be here, is the independent clause, while *who is my best friend* is the dependent clause and is a fragment.

Exercise
Place an *I* above the independent clause and underline twice and a *D* above the dependent clause and underline once.

1. Of the two sisters in the Smith family, Bob married the eldest.
2. Samantha, our lab director, is a very professional person.
3. She undoubtedly studied a great deal, when she was a student at university.
4. The man, who gave us the information, was tall and lean.
5. The crossing guard was barely taller than the children.

Answers
Listed below are the independent clauses; the parts of the sentences not listed are dependent clauses.

1. Bob married the eldest
2. Samantha is a very professional person.
3. She, undoubtedly, studied a great deal.
4. The man was tall and lean.
5. The crossing guard was barely taller.

Relative Pronouns and Antecedents

Words such as *than, which, who, whom, whoever, whomever, when, while,* etc., signal dependent clauses. They are called relative pronouns. They refer to other nouns in a sentence. So in number 4 in the previous exercise, the noun (man) that *who* is referring to is the antecedent. It comes before the pronoun *who*. (See the section on Pronouns.)

Titles

The title of a piece is the first thing a person sees, so it is important to choose an intriguing one. When you choose a topic, narrow it down to a specific idea behind it. Example: Topic: music. Topic sentence: Even though Beethoven and Shostakovich lived during different times, their music styles share some similarities.

Exercise
Think of three topics you might write about, and create interesting titles for them. Choose topics in which you are interested. Some might be: music, ethics, sports, exercise, diet, health, friendship, siblings, sharing, parents, dancing, hiking, goals, dream interpretation, gardening,

business behavior, success, child rearing, influence, psychology, mathematics, ecology, the brain, the universe, etc.. Discuss.

Capitalizing Titles
Example: *Gone with the Wind*
Always capitalize the first and last word, no matter what it is. Do not capitalize prepositions, conjunctions, or articles in the title.

Italics or Quotation Marks for Titles?
Italics or underline (We underline a title when we write in longhand, then translate it into italics when we type it

.

Book: *The Martian Chronicles*, <u>The Martian Chronicles</u>
Play: *Hamlet*, <u>Hamlet</u>
Magazine: *Southern Sierran*
CD: *Dengue Fever*
TV show: *The Big Bang Theory*
(Underlining is generally used only in school papers.)

Quotation marks
Chapter: "Rocket Summer"
Article: "Protecting the Planet"
Song: "Monsoon of Perfume"
TV show episode: "The Luminous Fish Effect"
Act and scene: "Act I", "Scene III"

The idea is that the larger piece is in italics, while the smaller piece, contained inside the larger piece, is in quotation marks. What do we do when a larger piece takes its title from a smaller piece?
Book: *The Breathing House*
Poem: "The Breathing House"

Exercise
Using the titles you created in the previous exercise under "Titles," put them in the proper format, similar to the examples above. Determine whether each title belongs to a book, an article, an episode, a scene, a screenplay, a movie, a tv show, a poem, or a song.

How to Create a Bibliography

Always check for the latest version of the Modern Language Association (MLA) handbook (or the style guide you are required to use). The MLA website, and almost any college or public library website, will have guidelines for creating a bibliography and writing a great essay.

When working on your essay/research, save the source information. I tell my students to save it on a USB drive and to email it to themselves, so they will be sure to have it. Then, you can paste it into the last page of your essay and create your bibliography. The bibliography can have many names, and all are a bit different: Works Cited, Notes, References, Sources, etc. There are the MLA, APA (*American Psychological Association*), CMA (*Chicago Manual of Style*), and other guidelines. Make sure you are using the format that the publisher, professor, or business requires. I began this book in MLA format, but iUniverse asked me to put it in CMA, which I have done. We do what is required.

When listing authors, use the last name first, then the first name of the first author. If there are other authors in the same entry, list their first and last names after the first author's name. Often, there is no author (as in a magazine or newspaper, because the staff does not always get credit or because several people worked on the piece).

Example:

Bibliography

Dyer, Wayne. *Living the Wisdom of the Tao*. Carlsbad: Hay House, Inc., 2008.
Author. Title. City: Publisher, Date.

The above citation is in MLA format and is for a common type of source (a book). It is important to adhere strictly to the format; otherwise, your work will not be taken seriously. For more, see "Works Cited, References, or Bibliography Sample Page" section of this book.

Exercise

Create your own bibliography using three different source type. Ex: book, website, newspaper. Discuss.

Layers of Errors

A student wrote the below introductory paragraph for an essay in my class. Rewrite it so that it is correct:

Incorrect original sentence:
In; My Name is Margaret, by Maya Angelou is based on learning to have dignity pride, and be strong about ones beliefs.
Since this sentence begins with *In*, it should mention what the author has done in the story.

Corrected sentence:
In her short story, "My Name is Margaret," Maya Angelou shows how her main character has learned to have dignity and pride. We see how Margaret learns to be strong in her beliefs.

I am not wild about the phrase "to be strong in her beliefs," but for a beginning writer's essay, it will do. The writer should also mention her source material (the book or website from which she got the short story), or she can include a bibliography at the end of her piece.

Short stories, chapters, pages on websites, songs, poems, and articles must have quotation marks (" ") around them. This is standard MLA practice and must appear on student and professional papers.

The section that says, "based on learning to have dignity pride, and be strong about ones [which should be *one's* because it is possessive] beliefs" does not work because it breaks the rule of *parallel structure*, which is discussed in depth in the "Parallel Structure" section of this book.

Oftentimes, one sentence will need to be rewritten, before it will make sense. Many people dislike rewriting, but even this book was rewritten, edited, and proofread before it went to print. We must correct any typos, language errors, illogical sequences, punctuation, and other errors that might appear.

Based on this one sentence above, I can tell that the student probably earned a C or a D grade, if she followed the pattern with which she started. We cannot afford to write like this in our everyday lives. Bosses, clients, and even friends do not take kindly to people who cannot write, whose pieces seem sloppy and unprepared.

Our Changing Language

When I was young, we spelled *color* as *colour* and *honor* as *honour*. These words are derived from French. Then people began to shorten them to *color* and **honor**. We still do spell *glamour* with its original spelling and *theatre* with the *tre* ending but not *centre*, which we now spell as *center*.

In the 1950s, there was no such word as *lite*, and a *site* was, and still is, a location on which a house would be built. Today, I see the word *through* spelled as *thru*, even by colleagues in memos, and am shocked to see it. It may be fine to spell it the short way for road signs (convenience and rapid comprehension) but not in regular correspondence.

Within the last three years, because some English person said *amongst,* and some American thought it sounded elegant, people began saying *amongst* instead of *among*. That is how language changes. We shall see if anyone begins using *whislt*. Now that I wrote it in this book, I will bet it catches on.

The past tense of the verb *hang* (as in hang a picture) is *hung*, but the past tense of *hang* (to suspend from the neck until dead) is *hanged*. This is one example of how the same word has a different twist.

People insist upon using old words in new ways, and they become the norm. New words are introduced into the language, and they too become the norm. Let's see if *bootylicious* sticks. It is now in the dictionary.

Some spellings have changed in the United States but are still spelled the same in Europe. Letters either have been removed or have changed positions. For example, *acknowledgement* (American) and *acknowledgment* (British) are both correct.

European spelling	*American spelling*
centre	center
theatre	theater , theatre
sceptre	scepter
favourite	favorite
colour	color
honour	honor
glamour	glamour (stayed the same)
harbour	harbor
manuover and manoeuvre (with the *oe* joined)	maneuver

Paragraphs

A paragraph is made up of a group of sentences that work together to reflect the main topic of that paragraph.

A sentence has one idea. A paragraph has one idea. An essay has one idea.

1. A sentences has one idea. A sentences is a group of words. It must have a subject and a verb and express a complete thought.

2. A paragraph has one idea. A paragraph can expand on one idea and end with the beginning of a new one, much like a TV show ends one idea, then begins with a surprise just before the commercial to make you come back for the next idea. This is called a "hook."

3. An essay has one idea. An essay (or article) usually can be boiled down to one overall topic, with details that reinforce that topic (idea).

Many students experience writer's block, because they do not trust that their own minds will get them to the essay. They can write a sentence, but they do not think they can string several sentences together to make a decent paragraph.

They can have a conversation that has many paragraphs in it, but they do not think they can *write* those paragraphs. Someone has taught them not to trust that the words will come. All these students need to do is to *begin writing*. They can fix the errors later.

Many teachers and books state that students must have a *therefore, moreover,* or some other transition word to move forward in a paragraph. This is not necessarily true. Such words can act as links between thoughts, but are not the only way to do so. When you are writing your *first* draft, just write what comes into your mind. Do not think about spelling, punctuation, or anything else. You just want get some ideas onto the page.

After writing your first complete draft, take a break from the piece. When you return to it, you will see it with a fresh view, and you can make your corrections and additions.

Students should write at least from three to five drafts of a piece in order to do a good job.

Exercise 1

Write your thoughts on the *value of education.* Do not judge what you write. Just write whatever comes out, whether it is a sentence, a word, or a paragraph. Trust the process. Mention your own or someone else's education or lack thereof. Mention characters in stories or things you imagine about education, real life, or anything at all.

Exercise 2

Circle your three favorite ideas from exercise 1. Keep your other ideas as a backup.

Exercise 3

Based on the three ideas you chose, create a first sentence for an essay that will discuss your main thoughts about the importance of education.
Discuss.

Writing Essays

There are numerous books, classes, and seminars on how to write essays. They all have one thing in common: they tell writers to be *clear.* Think of an essay as a magazine article. The reader will have no idea what you are discussing unless you tell him. When my students write an essay about Jeff Leeland's book, they cannot just say, "When Leeland talks about disabled children, it makes me sad." Readers will wonder, "Who is Leeland, and what is his complete name? What is this person talking about?" It is important to write complete thoughts in finished essays.

Exercise

Make a list of five topics that interest you. Example: 1. camping trips 2. ice hockey 3. travel 4. dating 5. making money

Trusting the Process, Generating Ideas

Many people criticize their own thoughts, sometimes before they even get onto the page. This is called "writer's block." It is okay, however, to allow those crazy "unacceptable" thoughts to come out. No one but you will see your first ideas. Your teacher or professor should not pressure you to share ideas that are very personal or that do not make sense. Idea making is supposed to be fun. Later, there will be time to judge and edit (get rid of errors and thoughts that don't work or might not be acceptable).

Free Writing

Many people begin by writing until they cannot think of anything else to write. That is called *free writing.* . There are also other strategies to help us fill in the blanks and create more order in your essays. The point of the exercises below is, not to do them perfectly, but to get a general idea of how to use each method, so you can keep them in your toolbox of ways to generate ideas for essays, articles, screenplays, and even books.

Exercise

Free write about the first topic you listed above. Keep writing until you run out of things to say. Discuss.

Brainstorming

Brainstorming is making a list of ideas related to a particular topic, choosing the best ones, and then putting them into a coherent order. This can be done before or after the free writing exercise.

Exercise

Brainstorm to develop three to five ideas your second chosen topic. Just write anything that enters your mind. Place them in some kind of order that makes sense to you. Discuss.

Clustering

To cluster is to make a circle in the middle of a page, and draw lines from that circle to topics that relate to it.

Exercise

Make a cluster of ideas for your third topic. Allow your mind to go free. Just write whatever you think about that topic. Highlight the three to five circles that best enlighten your reader about your topic. Discuss.

Outlining

An outline usually uses Roman numerals to organize the thoughts.

Exercise

Make a short outline of your fourth topic and ideas.

I. Hiking
   A. I enjoy hiking because it invigorates me.
      1. Great exercise
      2. Sunshine
      3. I can see the entire valley.

Discuss.

Using 3 x 5–inch Cards

Some people prefer to use 3 x 5–inch cards to organize their ideas.

Exercise

Use 3 x 5–inch cards to list ideas on your 5th topic. (or tear some paper into "cards"), and write your ideas on them. You can also just make a chart of boxes that represent cards and list one idea per "card" in each box. Discuss.

The Senses

Referring to the senses helps the reader really *feel and experience* what is happening.

Example 1:

At 5 p.m., Bob got a call from his girlfriend, Julie. She said, "My car broke down. I am here in Pasadena. Can you help?" He said, "I am watching the game. I can't come. Can't you call someone else?"

Example 2:

At 5 p.m., Syd got a call from Marian, his girlfriend. Tears streaming down her face, her voice trembling, she said, "My car broke down, and I was wondering …." Before she could finish her sentence, he grabbed his keys and said forcefully, "Where are you? Stay right there. I will be there in ten minutes."

It is clear right away who is the more caring man. The dialogue tells us what we need to know. The Bob-and-Julie scenario is not as descriptive as the Syd-and-Marian story. The senses are more involved in the Syd story. We *hear* them speaking to one another. We *see* the tears streaming down Marian's face. We do not need to be *told* who loves whom or who is the better man. We actually *experience* it. That is the power of using the senses in writing.

Here are some other examples:

1. The heat from the desert rose in ribbons of steam.

2. He could not help but turn as she passed, her skirt swinging and her spicy perfume remaining in his nostrils. He remembered the gentle touch of her hand.

3. Church bells ring as the fog mists over Juan, who meditates in the park.

4. She always despised the look, smell, and even the name of macaroni and cheese. Those disgusting, tight, little noodles stuck together with cheap cheese, two days old, that her mother had forced on her, even though she threw them up every time she ate them, were a horrible memory and represented all the abuse she had endured.

Pay attention to the world around you. See if you can add more descriptions using the senses in your creative and persuasive writing. Of course, this approach might not be appropriate in business writing.

Writing in Present Tense

The present tense makes the story more immediate. Many writers began writing in this style in the 1980s and became famous for it. This is not the only way to write, of course.

Changing Tenses in Essays

What is wrong with this sentence:
In 1986, David ran a marathon and <u>wins</u> the medal.

It should be:
In 1986, David ran a marathon and <u>won</u> the medal.

When it is necessary to change tenses, signal to the reader that it is happening. The example below is from a student essay about Alex, a sick child.

Incorrect:
The first blow to the family came in the form of blotches that seem to be spider bites. Days later, Alex comes down with a fever.

Correct:

The first blow to the family <u>came</u> in the form of blotches that <u>seemed</u> to be spider bites. Days later, Alex <u>came</u> down with a fever.

Since the writer began with the past tense, she must stay in the past, unless a change makes sense. For example, she might have said, *Now, Alex has come down with a fever* or written the entire section in present tense: The first blow to the family *comes* in the form of blotches that *seem* to be spider bites. Days later, Alex *comes* down with a fever.

Punctuation Tips

Apostrophes '
Apostrophes have a very important job. They show possession or when a letter or letters are missing, as in contractions. *Cannot* becomes *can't. He is* becomes *he's. Would have* becomes *would've.* (You should never use *would've* in formal writing.)

Colons :
Colons are similar to periods, but whatever follows them must relate to the previous sentence or section. Colons are not absolutely necessary in a sentence. When in doubt, use the punctuation you know how to use.

Incorrect:
Bob went to the store: When he was married to Kathy, he was very happy.
The store part has nothing to do with the marriage part.

Correct:
Bob went to the store. He bought the following: rice, steak, orange juice, and beans.

The horizontal format (the list follows the colon on the same line in the sentence) above is very commonly used. When making a long list or checklist, I prefer to use the vertical style used in this letter:

Dear Mr. Smith:

Thank you for our phone conversation. Enclosed is my résumé with the following:

Application
Résumé
BA transcripts
MA transcripts
Three letters of reference

We can number the list or use bullet points. Notice that in this formal letter I've used a colon instead of a comma after the recipient's name, because our relationship is formal

A colon can be used before a quotation, but usually, we use a comma.

Mary asked: "Did you get the milk?"

There are other uses for colons, but these are the most common.

Semicolons ;

Think of semicolons as stronger than a comma, but they do not stop the sentence like a period or colon would. They are excellent for lists that involve commas.

> The authors who will speak at the conference are Linda Hogan, reading from her book of poems, *The Book of Medicines*; Marcielle Brandler, discussing her poetry from *The Breathing House*; Deepak Chopra, demonstrating the concepts in his book, *The Path to Love*.

In the above example, there are commas between the authors and their works, and that is why we need semicolons to separate the authors from each other. An alternative approach is to organize them into separate sentences:

> Three authors will speak at the conference. Linda Hogan will read from her book of poems, *The Book of Medicines*. Marcielle Brandler will discuss her poetry from *The Breathing House*. Deepak Chopra will demonstrate the concepts in his book, *The Path to Love*.

When in doubt, do what you know. Now, you try it.

Exercise

Use semicolons to make a horizontal list using information of your choice or use the examples below.

1. From the cash register/ ten $50 bills/ nine $20 bills/ fifty $1 bills.
2. We spent $100 on clothes (name the clothes)/ $90 on food (name the foods)/ $30 on lunch (list what you ate).
3. My friends are: Mary, who is always helpful. Dave, who is the funniest person I know. Kate, who is my encyclopedia, because she knows almost everything.
4. In college, I studied: anthropology with Prof. Carl Parks. Music with Danielle Theroux. Spanish with Ezekiel Sepulveda.

Semicolons also are used between transitional words. For example:
I was running late; therefore, I could not get any cash from the ATM.
Some transitional words are: moreover, furthermore, however.

There are other uses for semicolons, but these are the most common.

Exercise

Write three sentences using semicolons and the transitional words listed above.

Commas ,

The comma seems to be the most troublesome punctuation mark. Seemingly subtle and used according to our personal judgment, it does employ very specific rules. The comma is not merely placed in a sentence when we take a breath. (Some of us take breaths more than others, as did Captain Kirk in *Star Trek*.) Commas indicate pauses for very definite purposes.

Commas in a series
This is the easiest use of commas: to divide ideas in a list. For example:
Mary had turkey, bread, pumpkin pie, and ice cream.
The comma before *and* in a series is optional in some circles; however, I would tell you to use it. *The Chicago Manual of Style* says to use it.

Exercise
Write sentences using these lists:
1. ham/tomatoes/glass of water/fried beans
2. walked to campus/bent down and tied my shoes/said hi to Bill
3. flowers everywhere/people nice all day/got extra pay

Commas before introductory phrases, parenthetical expressions, etc.
Introductory phrases:
No, I cannot be there. Because I want an education, I am attending college.

Parenthetical expressions:
I wish I could go, you know, but I have a job to do.

Appositives:
These are phrases that act as noun or pronoun. They tell you more about the subject.
Darrin, my best friend, is here.

Commas set off dates and places:
At 3 p.m. on March 10, 1995, I went to Toronto, Ontario, Canada.

Commas before quotations
Either a comma or a colon appears before dialogue.
Armine asked, "Will you give me a ride?"

In a play, you will see a colon after the character's name.
Marian: Stop that.

Parentheses ( )
Parentheses are for asides and separated information; they come either inside a sentence or after it.

Brackets [ ]
Brackets can be used inside when clarifying information to a quotation. For example, you are describing George Bush and Dick Cheney; then you quote someone: "He [Bush] declared war

on Iraq." Adding [Bush] within brackets lets the reader know that the writer was referring to Bush, not Cheney, even though the name was not used in that particular sentence.

Periods .

Periods end sentences and abbreviations.

Mary walked to the store.

Dr. John Smith

The US Postal Service (Now USPS is without a period.) has dropped the period at the end of abbreviations of states, so that you have *CA* for California (We still use *Calif.* for California.) and *UT* for Utah.

St. Louis still keeps the period.

Ellipses ...

Ellipses are used to show that words are missing in a sentence. There are only three dots, followed by whatever other punctuation is needed.

Deborah said that it would be fine to leave the cash at home ..., so let's do that.

This indicates that some information has been left out, perhaps something that distracts from the important part of the message.

Ending a sentence with an ellipse:

Deborah said that it would be fine to leave the cash at home, ...

There is an ellipse and a period, which is not preceded by an extra space.

The complete sentence is: *Deborah said that it would be fine to leave the cash at home, because it is a free event.*

If the writer were excited or asking a question, it would appear like this:

Deborah exclaimed, "It will be great to see you ...!"

Deborah asked, "Will it be all right to leave the cash at home ...?"

Both of the above could end with a period, unless the writer wants to make it clear that he is leaving out some text.

Italics *italics (slanted writing)*

Use italics to set a discussion apart. In novels and other works, they sometimes are used to represent the character's thoughts. They are also used to indicate the title of a book, website, play, screenplay, CD, movie, DVD, or any other complete piece.

Quotations Marks " "

We place quotation marks around quoted words, but there are other reasons to use them, such as to indicate sarcasm.

She "said" she would be there.

This shows that we doubt what she said.

We also use them for shorter pieces that appear as part of a larger piece. Names of poems, songs, chapters, episodes, and scenes are all enclosed by quotation marks.

Quotation marks are used to let the reader know that the writer is saying the exact words of the person whom he is quoting. Be sure you are accurate when quoting others. In certain states plagiarism is a felony. In others, it is a misdemeanor. That is why it is vital it is to quote and identify sources..

When we paraphrase, we are saying basically what the person said, but we are not using her exact words. We are doing more than summarizing, because we are covering almost everything the original author or speaker said. Do not use quotation marks when paraphrasing.

In my article, "Mind Control," I quoted, from memory, a visitor to a high school campus where I had taught. I neither remembered the speaker's name nor would have wished to reveal it had I known it, since what she said was disrespectful of the students. The following is what appeared in the article:

The lady said, "I know that many of you girls have short attention spans, but this film video I am about to show you does not have any statistics or words that you have to think about."
—"Mind Control," *Religion & Ethics Digest*, October 1996.

Quotation inside a quotation
Sometimes we quote someone who is quoting someone else. For example, this line appears in the book *Old Yeller* by Fred Gipson:
Mama laughed. "Well, Travis," she said, "it looks like we've got us a dog."

When I want to quote it in my essay, I will have to quote the quotation:
"Mama laughed. 'Well, Travis,' she said, 'it looks like we've got us a dog.'"

Notice that I begin with double quotation marks (" "), and for the inside quoted words, I use (' ') single quotation marks.

When my students and I did this exercise, we wrote:
David said, "It's a beautiful day."
Mary asked, "Did David say, 'It's a beautiful day'?"

Notice that Mary's statement ends with single and double quotation marks, and the question mark comes after David's comment. It looks strange, doesn't it?

The "Redundancies" section of this book includes the following:
"After Stephanie was introduced to the high school students, 'Everyone wanted to volunteer' (Leeland 145)."
I quoted a student who had quoted Jeff Leeland, so I used single quotation marks inside double quotation marks.

Rhetorical Forms

All of the forms listed below can be used in the same essay. We can use description in a narration; in fact, description is part of narration. We may wish to define something in a persuasive essay or discussion.

Narration

This is storytelling. Often, it is more effective to tell a story rather than to make your point some other way.

Definition

To define something is to make it real. In the 1970s, when I was twenty-one and newly married, my boss took me to his office and told me that my husband did not know how to please me, but that he (my boss) did. I left, never to return. Today, because there are now laws against sexual harassment, I could sue him. In those days, my only option was to quit my job. Sexual harassment is unwanted or inappropriate sexual attention.

Jihad is a commonly misunderstood word and needs to be defined more clearly. Oftentimes, the longer definition essay or article can clarify misunderstood concepts. See "jihad" in the "Definition" essay for further information on how a definition can change people's awareness about a certain word or idea.

Persuasion (Argument)

Persuasive essays, speeches, books, and discussions require the writer or speaker to make his case and "prove" that what he says is accurate. He must also answer to any counter argument an opponent may make. For example, we see how the below sentences lead towards certain conclusions:

All cats are feline.

This is a general statement and is obviously true; when we consult a dictionary, we find that the very definition of "cat" is to be "feline." We do not need to persuade anyone of the validity of the above statement. Be careful when you say "all" or "everyone," because there are usually exceptions to any such statement.

All cats are mean.

This can be easily disproven, but "some cats are mean," is probably true. It is possible to find an example of a mean cat.

When we wish to persuade, we must use credible sources. Using faith-based quotations such as from the Bible, Koran, Torah, Bhagavad gita, or other religious texts will persuade only those who agree that those sources are reliable. In scientific discussions, those sources will not hold up.

For example, this statement is not persuasive:
The Bible says that cats are mean.

What if the reader does not accept the Bible as a true source? You will lose your audience, and the reason you are writing the persuasive essay is to win readers to your side of the issue. At college, university, and among scholars, using faith-based arguments will lead to problems. Use researchable physically provable sources.

Then there is the logical train of thought. An example of this is:

Kind people do kind deeds.
Mary does kind deeds.
Therefore, Mary is a kind person.

You can learn more about this by looking on the web or in any critical thinking book under *inductive* and *deductive reasoning.*

Deductive reasoning moves from a general premise to a more specific conclusion.

Inductive reasoning moves from the particular to the general.

Exercise
Suggest a topic for a persuasive essay, then write three points that prove you are correct. Write one thing someone might say in disagreement and how you would counter his comment. Discuss with the class.

Process Analysis
In process analysis, a certain process or procedure is broken into steps that help explain the value of the process, why it does or does not work, or any other thought. Make sure you clearly state your understanding of the process and its result, which may be its usefulness or its lack thereof. It does not have to be an earth-shattering topic.

For example:
My cat, Maverick, is a great hunter.
In my description, I would explain how he hunts and the results.

Some possible topics:
1. Why Medicare is good or bad, or why it detracts from or adds to the quality of life in this country
2. Which musicians, teachers, friends, recreation areas, libraries, colleges, etc., are good or bad
3. Recipes
4. A how-to essay
5. Our social or political system
6. Health or healthcare

In making judgments, we must analyze what we are judging. We can discuss ideas that are abstract, but which should be able to be analyzed, for example, political, historical, social, or fashion movements or belief systems such as Christianity, Buddhism, existentialism (any of the isms).

Anything can be a process. Recipes and how-to essays involved process analysis. The digestive system or any system in the entire universe can be discussed in a process-analysis essay.

Exercise

Choose a topic for a process-analysis essay; then write down its steps and what you would say about it. Discuss with the class.

Description

We use the senses to describe a thing, idea, situation, or emotion. To describe makes a thing or situation more real. For example:

> Before I unlock the door, I hear his panting. As I enter the house, sparkly eyes make me glad I am there. His warm breath feels comforting after the cold outside, and his cozy fur invites me to hug him. Ooh, but what is that smell? He has pooped on the floor, and I need to air the place out.

I could get more detailed about the type of pooh smell or whether the dog has long clean hair or short spiky hair. Details in description make it more powerful and immediate.

"Touch" can happen with more than the fingertips. Remember, that the entire skin is the largest organ of the body. It is alive. An atmosphere bumps against our skin. The wind, a mood, a head rush, are all examples of things that touch.

"Smell" goes more deeply into our reptilian (at the base of the neck) part of the brain and our prehistoric memory than any of the other senses. A smell attracts, repels, angers, and excites.

Some things we could describe:
a campus
a home or room
a neighborhood
a person
a food
a situation
a job
your fantasy home, job, sweetheart
an object

There are numerous others.

Exercise

Choose one thing to describe. Under each of the five senses (see below), write a description of the thing you are describing. Then in a paragraph write a description using the list.

Taste
Smell
Touch
Hear
See

For Example

Many of us say or write, "For example …." To explain something to someone, and to ensure the person will understand, we use examples, which can be descriptions, statistics, quotations, stories or anecdotes, or any other rhetorical form. Read the below sentence:

> It has taken a great deal of work for Marcielle to write *Fun with Grammar.* She first had to get the education that would enable her to understand and absorb the concepts of English language usage. She then taught her subject for many years, after which she began writing the book, which also took several years.

Notice that the writer never said, "for example" or "an example of this is …" It is understood that everything following the first statement is an example. Within those two sentences are three examples.

Exercise

Write three statements, and add two examples for each one.

1. Statement
   a)
   b)
2. Statement
   a)
   b)
3. Statement
   a)
   b)

Division/Classification

We divide things, people, and ideas into classifications. You could also say that we classify the above into divisions. Our kitchen cabinets are divided into classes. All the food is in one section; then that section is divided into dry foods, then into cereals, pastas, coffees and hot chocolate mixes, etc. Similarly, the refrigerator is divided into sections as are the glassware and silverware. We divide ideas, people, places, and things, so that we can more easily work in and understand our world.

Examples include newspapers, offices, campuses, friendships, families, books, bookstores, websites, heroes, educations, types of people, ideas, emotions, belief systems, planetary systems, digestive system, animals, physical systems, psychological systems, etc.

I divided my friendships into levels. I have two best friends. One is female, and the other is male. I have an inner circle of a few very close and trusted friends. The ones who have really been there for me are inside the innermost part of the circle. While the others are close, they have not yet had a chance to prove themselves, although I may have proven my loyalty to them. I also have great friends with whom I do things and have lunch. The circle gets wider, and the friends become less and less intimate. There are four circles . We could call these the Inner/First, Second, Third, and Fourth Circles.

Exercise

List two things to classify, and divide them into their classifications and sub-classifications. For example:

Friendships
A. Inner/First Circle: closest friends
    1. Best friends: Two people; we always help each other.
    2. Dear friends: People who I trust but who have not had time to get to level one. I would feel comfortable asking them for help.
B. Second Circle
    1. Great people with whom I go to movies and lunches but whom I would not likely ask for help; not yet anyway. I help many of them, but they cannot help me.
C. Third Circle
    1. Nice people who accompany me to movies and lunches. I am unlikely to ask them for help. They are people to whom I am careful not to reveal certain things and with whom I have not established trust. I seldom see them. Some of them might have been in a closer circle at one time but betrayed my trust or have caused some other problem. Usually, these are people whom I help but who cannot or do not help me.
D. Fourth Circle: acquaintances

Exercise

Now, you try. Divide an idea or thing in any way you wish. It does not have to follow the example above.

1.
    a)
    b)

2.
    a)
    b)

Cause and Effect (Causal Analysis)

Everything has a cause, and we see the result as an effect. For example:
Bob is blind. The cause of this blindness is his diabetes, which has gotten out of control.

Many political and social analysis articles in newspapers, blogs, and magazines are cause/effect analyses. They ask, "Where are we, and how did we get here?" When we write such an essay, we can begin either with the effect or with the cause.

Beginning with the effect: *David has a fat stomach.*
Cause: *He never does sit ups or other exercises.*

Beginning with the cause: *David never does sit ups or other exercise.*
Effect: *Thus, David has a fat stomach.*

After you write your cause and effect, make a list adding more descriptions. For example:

Cause: David never does sit ups or other exercise. He used to be in shape because he rode his bike to work and played baseball with his little son. Now that his son has grown up and David drives a car to work, he no longer gets any exercise.

Effect: David has a fat stomach. He has a paunch that has grown larger and larger over the years. Because he does not fit into his nice clothes, he has stopped going dancing with his wife, and his knees are now beginning to buckle under his weight. He is depressed and feels sorry for himself.

Exercise
Now, you do it. Write a cause and its effect or an effect and its cause. Then list possible ideas under each topic. They could be solutions to a problem or the result of some issue. Discuss your thoughts.

Cause:
Effect:

Effect:
Cause:

Comparison/Contrast
We are constantly comparing and contrasting. When a student talks about her teacher, she might say, "Miss Jordan is such a great teacher, not like that Mr. Canton." The student will then go on to explain what makes Miss Jordan so good, and how she has contrasted this teacher with the one she does not like.

We see this in film. To make the hero look especially heroic, we must make the bad guy look very bad. The more evil the bad guy looks, the more the heroic the protagonist looks.

Compare = how two or more things or ideas are similar; for example, Mark is tall like Bob.

Contrast = how two or more things or ideas are different; for example, Mark is taller than Dale. Mark is five foot ten, and Dale is five foot five.

Topic ideas for comparing and contrasting
Police officers in Pasadena versus police officers in Watts
French versus Italian cooking, language, countryside, people, etc.
Laptop versus desktop computers
A certain game versus another
Marriage versus independence
Peanut butter versus almond butter
Strict parent versus lax parent
Good date versus bad date

Teachers and professors might want to brainstorm possible topics appropriate to your class for a wider range. This helps them to see that almost any topic is permissible, and that they do not have to choose something they either know nothing about, or a which does not interest them.

Often, the topics do not have much in common or they are not very different, so we might not be able to say much about them. For example, if Dale is similar to Mark, we can talk a great deal about their similarities, but not have much to say about their differences. Perhaps their differences are not important to the essay; if so, we do not need to focus on them.

Our essays do not necessarily have to be perfectly balanced (e.g., to compare three things and then contrast three things). As students, you must fulfill the assignments that are given to you, but as writers, you can choose how much attention to give a topic. Remember that even editors of journals, newspapers, and magazines have certain guidelines that you must follow.

In order to generate ideas, I might make a chart like the one below. These are my perceptions of two great actresses.

Marilyn Monroe	Hedy Lamarr
Actress	Actress/Producer/Scientist/Inventor
Insecure/childlike	Very confident/mature persona
Blonde	Dark haired
Often silly	Always serious
American born	Austrian born
Open	Mysterious

Exercise
Using either a chart or by free writing:
Compare two people, things, or ideas.
Contrast two people, things, or ideas.

Critique or Review
A critique of what someone else has said or accomplished must be done with care. You do not want to appear disrespectful or biased.

Things to critique: book, CD, DVD, movie, performance, article, music, speech, seminar.

Where critiques often appear: newspapers and magazines have sections in which readers can comment on articles from the last edition. They have also articles discussing and reviewing performances of dance troupes, orchestras, plays, etc.

Websites that sell books, etc., often have sections in which customers can critique or review someone's work.

Many blogs critique performances and other people's work.

My website (http://www.webspawner.com/users/marcielle/) has many critiques, some written by my students and others by me. One that I wrote years ago and posted on Amazon.com is called, "Salma Kahlo." (See "Works Cited" section for more information.) Critiques do not have to be positive. You may dislike a piece, and you have the right to express that displeasure. My website includes a review that I wrote of a Kevin Kline film ; it is called "Enigmatic Emperors." I explained how disappointed I was with the film, while praising the areas I thought were praiseworthy. You do not have to choose just one side. You might be divided in your feelings as I am below:

"Enigmatic Emperors"

The Emperor's Club starring Kevin Kline was quite a good story, but the writers missed a great opportunity to inform and surprise the viewer. Kline's character teaches at an exclusive all-boy's school and uses the emperors of ancient Rome as examples of how one obtains greatness. The problem is that he never lets the audience know any of the great accomplishments of the supposedly great men. He says several times that greatness without contribution is meaningless. A plaque over the professor's classroom door mentions the name of an ancient king who no one supposedly ever heard of, yet his name has survived centuries and is mentioned in this film. One also wonders what Caligula and Nero contributed to mankind, yet they are remembered. I also wanted to hear exactly what does make an honorable man. The film was pleasant enough, but it lacked fullness, layers.

Maybe because I was raised in the fifties (an era in which we were given moral stories in our films, TV shows, and at school as well as home) I expect the answer to the question, "What exactly makes an ethical person?" complete with illustrations. I was so looking forward to being inspired by this film. I did enjoy the lesson the professor learns about life and responsibility and that it is not merely one act that makes or breaks a "man," but a lifetime of small acts. I appreciated his and his students' struggles.

I just wanted to see more personal interaction between him and the students with him modeling honorable behaviors. Instead, the only time the professor does make a mistake, he does exactly what he should not do. He runs from responsibility when he breaks the car window of the school's dean. That was completely out of character. I, and others I spoke to, did not believe that the professor would do that, unless he were a hypocrite, which that scene makes him out to be. This was an opportunity for him to walk calmly to his dean's car and say, "I broke your window. I am terribly sorry. I will pay for the cost of repairs."

Kline's character ages very realistically. [The film] was neither overacted nor was the makeup overdone. I flashed back on teacher-student stories like *To Sir with Love, Room 222, Blackboard Jungle*, and *Dead Poets' Society*, all very different, and all revealing aspects of teaching of which the public has little idea. I am glad there is a new TV series called *Boston Public* that shows the gritty side of teaching. Having taught all grades and now college, I appreciate both the raw and the genteel aspects of the profession. In both settings, educators are given the responsibility to teach morals. *The Emperor's Club* attempts to do the same but falls a bit short.

Exercise
Think of a movie, book, or performance you have seen that you would like to critique. Write three specific things about it. Discuss.

Title:
1.
3.
3.

Symbols versus Words

A symbol is an image, object or anything else that represents an idea or another thing. For example, the Olympic rings represent the five continents involved in the Olympics.

A metaphor is a comparison between two things.

Example:
"Juliet is the East." –Romeo in Shakespeare's, *Romeo and Juliet*
Romeo calls Juliet the East, because the sun rises in her. In other words, she is the source of light.

Sometimes a metaphor or symbol can be extremely powerful and have a greater impact on a reader, viewer, or listener than an explanation, especially when it comes to abstract ideas. A metaphor is an image, word, or phrase that represents something else.

For example, when we see a swastika, we assume that it is connected to the Nazi regeim of Adolf Hitler's Germany. Of course, the swastika has other meanings and is an ancient symbol which has been used by Native Americans, Greeks, Hindus, and others for good purposes.

The Honda symbol represents the Honda brand. It may have a deeper meaning that the public is not aware of.

A family crest is another type of symbol.

The words, *patriot, mother, love,* etc. have become symbolic and have a great deal of meaning attached to them.

People can be symbols. Martin Luther King Jr., Gandhi, and Donald Trump all represent certain ideas.

An action can be symbolic. When Tita, the main character in the novel, *Like Water for Chocolate*, by Laura Esquivel, knits a blanket, she does so while the man she loves is in his marriage bed with Tita's sister. Later, the blanket becomes a symbol of all Tita's lonely nights. The author avoids stating outright how lonely Tita has been, but when we see how huge the blanket is, we *feel* her many nights of pain.

Note: You can find many symbols on the World Wide Web. See *Google Images* for best results.

Exercise
Draw three symbols that exist in our world. Discuss what they mean.

Create your own logo or symbol, and tell the class what it means.

Critique/Review or Process Analysis in Responding to Another Person's Work
Many people begin writing (free writing) before planning their essays. That may work, but we should follow a few guidelines, such as the ones below. This list assumes that you have read a book or article and wish to discuss it.

1. Always introduce the title, author, and source you are critiquing in your first paragraph, often in the first sentence. For formal essays, you will create a bibliography.

2. Discuss the purpose of the author's essay and, perhaps, how you assessed that purpose. Explain what is correct or incorrect about the author's goal or logic.

3. Tell the reader what the author is describing or what his process is in evaluating the text. How do you think the author has arrived at his conclusions? Do you agree or disagree with his conclusions or premises? Why or why not? Add your thoughts. Do there need to be more steps in the author's analysis? Is the author missing something? Why are your additional steps important? How do the steps help the reader to understand the process more clearly? What would others say about the steps, and how would you counter their comments?

4. You may wish to introduce an outside source (which you must cite; see definition of "cite" below). to empower your own words. What does that person have to say about the topic mentioned in the essay? What is that person's position? If he is a specialist in a certain field, readers need to know that. This will give his words more punch, more authority.

5. It is always good to quote at least once from the essay you are analyzing. Note: When we cite a source, we are giving readers the information they need to find the source. See the section below called "With a 'Works Cited' page."

Exercise
Now that you have written ideas about a movie, book, or performance you have seen, introduce it. You may wish to refer to the above, "Enigmatic Emperors" article from the "Critique or Review" portion of this book, as a guide.

A Way to Begin an Essay on a Poem
Poetry can be a challenge. Many instructors have very specific ideas of what a particular piece of literature might mean, and when students stray from their teachers' ideas or what research has revealed, poor grades often are the result. I allow my beginning students to say what they feel about a poem, as long as they can back up their ideas..

Each student must make a logical case for his interpretation. Often, it is radically different from what I had intended, but since they are exploring and making the attempt, I give them credit for their work.

Below are two poems, one very easy and the other more challenging. See if you can say three interesting things about each one.

"What the Ugly Boy and the Pretty Girl Have in Common"

She is stared at.
His face is passed over.
Neither of them are seen.
She's so cute, it's assumed she's spoiled.
He's so ugly, he's cute.
He can't believe she likes him.
She's afraid he'll find something he doesn't like.
They marry.
Over the years, his face acquires dignity,
and her face gains character.
Now, people say how alike they look.

"Eden"

I startled my mother in the blazing
hallway, her breasts an exotic gift
my lips had never suckled. It was

an accident we met. Never before
had I beheld anyone naked. My sisters
told me of the times they had watched

her. I imagine my mother lifting
herself from the forgiving floral suds
of her bath. This secret time I had

never visualized until now. She glides
on her hose, attaching them with
little posy snaps, and perfumes

herself in her personal
scent. Slithering into her
strapless cocktail dress, her

shoulders glowing, she fluffs up
her hair like a delicate fern,
then entwines the glittering

necklace and presses on the blossom
lipstick which my father will kiss
from her mouth before they

lie down in the room where only they

may sleep. What are these angry wings
barring me from her garden? I remember

the last time she bathed me. I was
five and embarrassed. I turned away,
and she left me in my
unscented water.

Exercise
Answer the questions below. Trust your own thoughts. Allow yourself to think freely about these poems. There are no absolute right or wrong answers.

"Ugly Boy/Pretty Girl"
1. What does "neither of them are seen" mean to you?
2. How is she perceived? Why? Is it always true either in the poem or in real life?
3. How is he perceived? Why? Is it always true either in the poem or in real life?

"Eden"
1. What does the title have to do with the girl in the poem?
2. Her sisters have more access to her mother than she does? Why is access to one's mother important to a child? What could not having a closeness with one's mother feel like?
3. Whose "angry wings" are keeping her from the garden? (Hint: Think about the "Adam and Eve" story in the Bible.)

After thinking about these poems, begin writing about them and forming your essay. Remember that there are other sources to which you can refer. You can do a search on any topic in the poem and even on how to critique a poem. Instructors will be impressed if you put extra work into a piece. Always have a works cited page for your sources, or at least mention the sources. (See sections on works cited pages, below.)

Some ideas for topics to research regarding these poems:
Beauty
Popularity
Family loyalty
Mother/daughter relations
A child's unconditional love for a parent.
Symbols in the Garden of Eden story
Marriage bonds
Can never go back to the past, "Eden."

Without a "Works Cited" Page
You can write an essay that does not have a works cited page. When you do that, mention the source right after the quotation or paraphrase. It is vital to do that, so the reader knows where to look for the piece on his own. Mention the author, title of piece from which you are quoting, and the source. This example includes a poet, her poem, the book title, and the publisher:

Linda Hogan's poem "Bear," from her book of poems, *The Book of Medicines*

(Coffee House Press), is a startling example of simplicity and stark metaphor. Her line, "The bear is a dark continent that walks upright," reveals that there is another world in this animal that is foreign to us. We too walk upright …

Then, the writer continues to discuss the metaphors in "Bear," using examples, comparisons, and whatever else applies, just as she would for a short story or an article.

With a "Works Cited" Page

This is the preferable format for all essays, articles, books, and even websites. You will notice that this book, *Fun with Grammar*, has a "Works Cited" section. It signals to readers that you have done your research and are quoting from actual sources. Of course, this does not mean that you should trust all books, essays, articles, speeches, and websites. (More on this is included in the "Should We Trust Every Source?" section.) We all have our biases, but at least we can let our readers know that we are backing up our claims using sources other than ourselves.

> Linda Hogan's poem "Bear" is a startling example of simplicity and stark metaphor. Her line, "The bear is a dark continent that walks upright," reveals that there is another world in this animal that is foreign to us. We too walk upright …

Then, we will discuss the metaphors in "Bear," using examples, comparisons, and whatever else applies, just as we would for a short story or article. The sources of the quotations, including the book titled *The Book of Medicines*, will be listed under "Works Cited."

Do not put quotation marks around "Works Cited" in the actual manuscript, only when it is referred to in another text. I did so in the above sentence, because I was referring to it. (See "Titles" section.)

Last page of essay

The last page usually includes the "Works Cited" section, for example:

Works Cited

Hogan, Linda. *The Book of Medicines*. Minneapolis: Coffee House Press, 1993.

For more information on the above topic, see the "How to Create a Bibliography" section.

Works Cited versus Bibliography

"If you are undertaking academic study at an English speaking institution or university, then it is important that you understand the difference between works cited and a bibliography. Depending on the professor's course requirements you will be required to produce both of them accurately as part of your assignment and essay work.

In general a works cited is a smaller list than a bibliography. When producing a works cited for an essay you only list the actual sources of information that you referenced in your piece of work. A bibliography, on the other hand, lists all the works and sources of information that you consulted while undertaking research into your paper."

—"Difference Between Works Cited and Bibliography"

A works cited list and a bibliography are not the same thing. A works cited list includes only items that have actually quoted. A bibliography lists all of the material consulted whether or not it was cited in the essay.

Put entries in works cited, references, or bibliography sections in alphabetical order by last names of authors, editors, translators, etc., or by the first words of titles if there is no author.

If the first word of the title is "The," "A," or "An," and the word is being used as an article. For example, in the title *The Little Book of Irish Clans*, the entry is placed under "Little" and the article "the" is ignored. In the title *A Is for Apple*, however, the entry is placed under "a" since it is used as a noun and not as an article in this case.

Sometimes "the" is used as part of the name of a company or periodical for emphasis, as in *The Champ* or *The Sports Network*. When citing Internet sites, use the URL as a guide. If "the yellow pages" is used in the URL, treat "the" as part of the title, and list "The Yellow Pages" alphabetically under "the." If "edge" and not "the edge" is used in the URL, list the magazine title *The Edge* under "edge" and ignore the article. Where appropriate, use a cross-reference to direct readers to the proper location, for example:

Yellow Pages, The see The Yellow Pages

References versus Sources
A "Works Cited" is sometimes referred to as "References." The terms mean the same thing. Each is an alphabetical list of works that were either cited or referenced. "Works Cited" is generally used with MLA style, while "References" is used with APA style.

Remember:
1. Do not numbered entries. Those are for "Footnotes."

2. Do not list citations separately by categories. All references should be placed in one list, alphabetized by the first words in the citations, regardless of where citations come from.

3. Begin on a new page. Start on the sixth line from the top (or one inch down from the top of the paper), center, and type one of the following titles: Works Cited, References, or Bibliography. Double space after the title. List all entries in alphabetical order by the first word, taking into consideration the rules for dealing with articles.

4. Begin the first line of each entry flush at the left margin. Keep typing until you run out of room at the end of the line. Indent five spaces for second and subsequent lines of the same entry. Double-space all lines, both within and between entries. Remember that these guidelines are adapted from the MLA Handbook. Follow the style recommended by your instructor.

Works Cited, References, or Bibliography Sample Pages

Online Articles
"Citing Online Sources," *MLA Handbook*
Elements (with samples):

1. Author's name (last name, first name): Kass, Leon R.

2. Title of article (in quotation marks): "Defending Human Dignity"

3. Name of periodical (italicized): *Commentary*
   Note: No period follows the title.

4. Volume and issue numbers: 124.5
   Note: Journal citations always include the volume and issue number while magazine citations do not.

5. Date of publication in parentheses: (2007)

6. Page number(s): 53–61.

7. Database title (italicized): *Expanded Academic ASAP*

8. Medium of publication: web

9. Date of access (your visit to site): 31 Aug. 2009

Formula:
Author. "Title of Article." *Name of Periodical* Volume. Issue. (Date published): Page Number(s). *Database Title*. Medium of publication consulted. Date of access. Indent the second line five spaces. Double space.

Examples:
Kass, Leon R. "Defending Human Dignity." *Commentary* 124.5 (2007): 53–61.

   Expanded Academic ASAP. Web. 31 Aug. 2009.

Loos, Ryland. "Hunting Animals Is Morally Acceptable." *Opposing Viewpoints: Animal*

   Rights. Ed. Andrew Harnack. San Diego: Greenhaven Press, 1996: n. pag. *Opposing*

   Viewpoints Resource Center. Web. 31 Aug. 2009.

Martinez, Al. "Things That Go Buzz in the Night." *Los Angeles Times* 11 Apr. 1999: 1.

ProQuest Newspapers. Web. 31 Aug. 2009.

Nolte, Carl. "A City and Its Firemen Mourn Their Fallen Comrade." *The San Francisco Chronicle* 31 Oct. 2003: A18+. *LexisNexis Academic*. Web. 31 Aug. 2009.

Price, Tom. "Future of Journalism." *CQ Researcher* 27 Mar. 2009: 273–96. *CQ Researcher Online*. Web. 31 Aug. 2009.

Reyes, Sonia. "Fighting the FAT Backlash." *Brandweek* 5 May 2003: 24+. *Expanded Academic ASAP*. Web. 31 Aug. 2009.

See *OWL Purdue Online Writing Lab*. "MLA Sample Works Cited Page."

Online Books

Note: If citing an online book that also appeared in print, begin the citation with the relevant facts about print publication (author(s), editor(s), title, place of publication, publisher, year published, etc.), followed by:

1. Title of the database or website (italicized)
2. Medium of publication consulted: web
3. Date of access (day, month, and year)

Examples:

Berk, Laura E. *Awakening Children's Minds: How Parents and Teachers Can Make a Difference*. New York: Oxford UP, 2004. *NetLibrary*. Web. 4 Sep. 2009.

LaPensee, Kenneth. "Vaccines and Vaccine Development." *Infectious Diseases: In Context*. Ed. Brenda Wilmoth Lerner and K. Lee Lerner. Vol. 2. Detroit: Thomson Gale, 2008. *Gale Virtual Reference Library*. Web. 4 Sept. 2009.

Web Pages

Note: A web page is a single document on the World Wide Web, a part of a website. It can be compared to online version of an article or a section of a book.

Elements:
1. Name of the author, compiler, editor, or translator: Green, Joshua.
2. Title of the web page or article (in quotation marks): "The Rove Presidency."
3. Title of the overall website or online periodical (*italicized*): *The Atlantic.com*.
4. Version or edition used (if any): [none given]

5. Name of the sponsoring institution or publisher, followed by comma: Atlantic Monthly Group,

6. Date of publication or latest update: Sept. 2007.

7. Medium of publication: web.

8. Date of access (your visit to site): 8 Sept. 2009.

9. URL <http://www.theatlantic.com/doc/200709/karl-rove>.

Note: Include a URL as supplementary information only when the reader would not be able to locate the source without it or if the instructor requires it.

Formula:

Author/s. "Title of the page." *Title of the website*. Version or edition used [if any]. Name of sponsoring institution, date of publication. Medium of publication. Date of access. <URL optional, ask your instructor>.

Examples:

Green, Joshua. "The Rove Presidency." *The Atlantic.com*. Atlantic Monthly Group, Sept.

2007. Web. 8 Sept. 2009. <http://www.theatlantic.com/doc/200709/karl-rove>.

Henderson, Wade. "Unfinished Business." *Civil Rights Today*. Voices of Civil Rights,

Apr. 2004. Web. 8 Sept. 2009. <http://www.voicesofcivilrights.org/civil2.html>.

Tyre, Peg. "Standardized Tests in College?" *Newsweek.com*. Newsweek, 16 Nov. 2007.

Web. 8 Sept. 2009. <http://www.newsweek.com/id/70750>.

Van Helden, Albert et al., eds. "Copernican System." *The Galileo Project*. Rice

University, 1995. Web. 8 Sept. 2009.

<http://galileo.rice.edu/sci/theories/copernican_system.html>.

Revised Sep. 2009 by B. Vasquez, D. Fuhrmann and A. Mezynski.
Double spacing provided by Fun with Grammar for easier reading.

The above list is from the Los Angeles City College Library website. See "Works Cited."

Should We Trust Every Source?

Most college and university campuses as well as libraries now have online resources that students and scholars can use to do research. They include newspapers, journals, and magazines that librarians all over the country have handpicked as reliable sources. If someone merely does a search for a subject online, he might arrive at a biased or disreputable website.

Searching on Google for Martin Luther King is commonly used as an example. Students may reach a very racist site that is cleverly disguised as informative information that reveals King's true story. A few clicks into the site reveals instead that the Grand Wizard of the Ku Klux

Klan is the source for the information. If the researcher does not know who this man is, she might believe what she reads on the site and use it as a credible source.

Many sites are created as a way to sell a product. Their authors will appear in online and hard-copy magazines as experts on a particular topic. They will convince the reader that he needs their product and suggest it is the only real solution. That is why the university and library online resources, which cost a great deal of money, have been set up at no cost to us. I encourage you to use them. Ask your librarian for guidance. Librarians are extremely helpful.

Exercise
List three sources that you believe are not reliable. They do not have to be online sources. Discuss.

List three sources that you believe are reliable. Discuss.

Partner Sheet
The below "Partner Sheet" is a tool students use to analyze one another's essays.
This sheet can be used by students or writers who have completed a best draft and want the insight of another student/writer. I require that students use a "Partner Sheet" for every essay they write in my classes. You can copy and paste it into a document and have your partner fill it out as she reads your best draft. You should do the same for your partner. Then you can use the comments on the sheet to make adjustments in your essay.

Partner Sheet

Your name:_____

Your partner must answer these questions for you while you fill out the sheet. Or your partner can fill out the sheet.

1. Partner's first name:

2. What she or he thinks your topic is:

3. How does the rough draft begin?

4. Can the reader tell how the writer feels about the issue? Explain why or why not.

5. If the writer can come up with more proofs or examples to explain his/her point of view, what would they be?

a)

b)

c)

6. If the writer already has good proofs or examples to explain his/her point of view, what are they?

a)

b)

c)

7. How does the author end the essay? For example, with a quotation, by calling readers to action, or other method, etc.

8. If this essay has a good ending, say why. If it is not, give an alternative.

A Source that Has Been Questioned

A very popular book is circulating among New Thought people (Those who study the Law of Attraction, or are affiliated with the Unity and Religious Science churches) called *The Hidden Messages in Water*. The author, Dr. Masaru Emoto, claims that he did research on water crystals. He says that he put labels on water bottles with various words or phrases. He let them sit over night, then observed the water crystals under the microscope. Depending on the emotion evoked by a word or phrase, the crystal would organize itself. If he used the phrase, "Thank you," the crystals would be perfectly formed, but if he used the phrase "You fool," the crystals did not form.

I wanted to trust his "research," but he lost me when he showed a picture of a man with a gun and later a baby's face. After that, I was even more suspicious of his "findings," so I did an Internet search and found the article below. This is what we need to do. We need to think for ourselves (i.e., critically, in order to discover the truth).

"Are Dr. Masaru Emoto's Fantastic Claims Actually Real?"

When I first heard of Dr. Emoto's amazing work with water crystals through his book "The Hidden Messages in Water" I was absolutely stunned. I then saw the movie "What the Bleep do we Know" and became thoroughly intrigued. I set off to conduct a research project in the chemistry department of Castleton College in Vermont to see if I could find sufficient evidence and support for Dr. Emoto's claims to merit conducting a deeper research project to try to reproduce his work. The idea was to uncover as much information about his methods and procedures as possible to determine if [it] would actually be feasible to study the effect of energy healing, such as Reiki, on the formation of water crystals. I was so excited to think that I might be the first person in the world to verify his work!

So what follows is my official research paper that contains all of my findings and determinations after months of exhaustive review of Dr. Emoto's published works. I hope that it will give you a deeper understanding and appreciation for the truth.

Sincerely,
Kristopher Setchfield, BA, Health Science
Natural Science Department
Castleton State College, Vermont (With author's permission.).

… While it is possible that he did, in fact, discover that water has an observable sensitivity to external stimuli such as prayer and words, Dr. Emoto's experimental design and clinical procedures do not prove the claim. A double blind procedure in which a photographer would not know what water sample he or she was photographing would make the claim considerably more credible.

Emoto's procedure, while simple and direct, does not eliminate numerous possible sources of error. Ice crystal structural formation is dependent on numerous environmental factors, the most important of which are temperature and humidity. While Emoto minimized some possible sources of error by conducting his studies in the same room with the same sample sizes, the same freezer and same microscope each time, other possible sources of error were not addressed. For example the Petri dishes were not sealed to prevent contamination or disturbance by the operator or environment; A simple thing such as the photographer's breath while using the microscope could affect the warming rate of the frozen sample and temperature of crystal formation, thus affecting the structure of the resultant crystal.

As Dr. Emoto has not published the entirety of his photographs, it is unknown if he ruled out or ignored crystals that did not support his hypothesis. HMW and the JACM article only contain selected photos that support his claims, and we are left to wonder what the rest of the pictures look like. His procedures state that in any given test he will photograph 100 petri dish samples, yet only one picture per test is provided to the public. Emoto also fails to publish any findings that contradict his claim (or that were at least inconclusive). No errors are currently published in the JACM article, his websites, or his HMW book that my research has been able to uncover. It is also worth noting that Dr. Emoto's procedures indicate that his samples are frozen at -25°C, and his ice crystals are formed at -5°C. According to Figure 3, these temperatures should produce mostly column crystals rather than plate crystals, yet not one of Emoto's published photos show a column crystal. This makes Dr. Emoto's data suspect (as they appear to conflict with the findings of well-respected researcher) and indicates the possibility that Emoto excluded non-supportive data from his publications.

While Emoto has published his claim in one peer reviewed journal, it has neither been substantiated nor disproved by research scientists. It is worth noting that Emoto's Journal article is not a scientific report, but a three page long "photo essay." Dr. Emoto, himself, stated "Even though my book, *Message from Water*, was first published in 1999 and has been translated in over 20 languages, I have not heard of anybody else conducting similar research" (Woodhouse). His claims resonate with "Alternative therapists, religious leaders, spiritual researchers, artists, and musicians" (Emoto, Healing 3), but it appears that his work has widely been disregarded by traditional scientists as pseudoscience that does not merit further inspection.

     -With permission by author.

If you visit Setchfield's website, you'll notice that he has a "Works Cited" page. That is one of the very important things a researcher like you should look for. He also has cited Emoto's words in his own article and refutes (questions/disagrees with) it directly. He employs the words of other researchers on the same topic and offers what they have said to bolster his own conclusions.

When a scientist makes a claim, she usually publishes it in a scholarly journal and other scientists support or refute it. That is another clue for a person doing research. We must ask ourselves, *Who else has done a study on this topic and what are the findings?*

Exercise
Find a piece of writing that makes a claim, and do some research on it. Write a brief paper with your own findings. Make a "Works Cited page," and quote from the first source and from sources who refute the author's claims.

Definition Essay
As discussed in the "Rhetorical Forms" section, a *definition* essay illucidates an idea and gives in-depth information to help the reader better understand it. Make sure you go to the right source (not to hearsay) for your information. For example, "jihad" is one of the most misunderstood words to English-speaking people, so it is a good topic to define. Below is an article from the internet that defines jihad from the perspective of those who actually teach and practice it.

Guidance from the Holy Qur'an

"Jihad: Supreme Efforts in the Way of Allah"

Jihad means exerting one's utmost power contending with an object of disapprobation, and this is of three kinds, namely (1) with a visible enemy, (2) with Satan, and (3) with one's self.

The Qur'an teaches that when war breaks out, it should be waged in such a way as to cause the least possible amount of damage to life and property; and that hostilities should be brought to a close as quickly as possible.

22:40 Permission to *fight* is given to those against whom war is made, because they have been wronged—and Allah indeed has power to help them.

22:41 Those who have been driven out from their homes unjustly only because they said, "Our Lord is Allah." And if Allah did not repel some men by means of others, there would surely have been pulled down cloisters and churches and synagogues and mosques, wherein the name of Allah is oft commemorated. And Allah will surely help one who helps Him. Allah is indeed Powerful, Mighty.

60:9 Allah forbids you not, respecting those who have not fought against you on account of *your* religion, and who have not driven you forth from your homes, that you be kind to them and act equitably towards them; surely Allah loves those who are equitable.

60:10 Allah only forbids you—respecting those who have fought against you on account of *your* religion, and have driven you out of your homes, and have helped *others* in driving you out, that you make friends of them, and whosoever makes friends of them—it is these that are the transgressors.

61:11 O ye who believe! shall I point out to you a bargain that will save you from a painful punishment?

61:12 That you believe in Allah and His Messenger, and strive in the cause of Allah with your wealth and your persons. That is better for you, if you did not know.

29:70 And as *for* those who strive in Our path—We will surely guide them in Our ways. And verily Allah is with those who do good.

9:20 Those who believe and emigrate *from their homes for the sake of God* and strive in the cause of Allah with their property and their persons have the highest rank in the sight of Allah. And it is they who shall triumph.

9:111 Surely, Allah has purchased of the believers their persons and their property in return for the Garden they shall have; they fight in the cause of Allah, and they slay and are slain—*a promise that He has made* incumbent on Himself in the Torah, and the Gospel, and the Qur'an. And who is more faithful to his promise than Allah? Rejoice, then, in your bargain which you have made with Him; and that it is which is the supreme triumph.

4:96 Those of the believers who sit *still*, excepting the disabled ones, and those who strive in the cause of Allah with their wealth and their persons, are not equal. Allah has exalted in rank those who strive with their wealth

and their persons above those who sit *still*. And to each Allah has promised good. And Allah has exalted those who strive above those who sit *still*, by a great reward.
—From *Selected Verses of the Holy Qur'an*

Exercise
List three ideas about jihad from the above article, without adding your own opinions. Discuss.

Write a definition essay using one of the topics listed below. What must it have or not have? Discuss.

Possible topics:
sexual harassment
kindness
friendship
honesty
patriotism
intelligence

Letters, E-mails, and Phone Calls: Business and Personal

All letters, e-mails, and even conversations can end up in court or on your boss's desk as legal evidence. Conversations cannot easily be proven, but the written word can; therefore, it behooves us to take care with our words, as they can be used for or against us later. Before sending out that angry letter in which you have called someone a name and threatened her, go back and reword it into a polite and formal request.

An *informal letter* is one in which the writer and receiver are conducting business or who know one another personally. It can be considered a "friendly" letter. These are letters to friends, loved one, and acquaintances that are written in a relaxed manner.

A *formal letter* is correspondence that the writer intends to communicate in a business-like manner.

Informal letters can have the date and name of the person to whom you are writing with your signature or just your name at the end.

Exercise
Create an informal letter or e-mail to a friend. Discuss.

Sample Letter to Sue Someone in Small Claims Court
Note: Remember to look up the latest rules and laws on this topic. This is not intended to constitute legal advice but to guide students in proper writing skills.

Format
First, create a letterhead at the top of the letter. It should include your name, address, and phone number. Many people include their e-mail addresses as well. Save every e-mail, letter,

or any other correspondence between you and the other person, so the judge can examine them or just for your records. Be sure to make two copies; one for you and one for the judge for your court date.

Contents

In any request letter, state clearly what was agreed upon, what happened, and what you now expect. Avoid unnecessary detail about how hurt you were by the other person's behavior. Two examples are given below: an incorrect letter and a corrected version. The characters in these letters are hypothetical and not real people.

> Mary,
>
> I thought we were friends. I am so upset. Before I did all that babysitting, you would always answer my calls, and now just because you owe me that money, you never even call. You are such a jerk. Don't ever expect to hear from me again.
>
> Julie

The letter above does not have a letterhead, the person's full name and address, or even the date. She does not mention the amount of money that Mary owes her, what she wants, or when she wants it.

Below is what Julie should have written. Notice that this letter uses their formal names. It states clearly and concisely what happened and what did not happen. It puts Mary on notice and gives her an exact date by which she should send the full payment.

> Julie Gardner
> Address
> City, CA, 90000   Telephone & Fax
>   E-mail address
>
> _____
>
> Mary Smith
> Address
> City, state, zip
>
> April 1, 2007
>
> Dear Mary Smith:
>
> On March 1, 2007, you hired me to baby sit your two children, Carmen and Josie, over the weekend, while you and your husband went on an anniversary trip to Hawaii. You said you would pay me $300.00 for doing this.
>
> I took care of your children in my home. I fed, bathed, and entertained them

during this time, which took my entire weekend, and during which I had to put my life on hold.

Upon your return, you promised to give me a check for the agreed-upon amount, but you have not done so. I have called and e-mailed you several times, but you have not answered the phone or e-mails. Now, a month later, I am letting you know that if I do not receive my money and have the check clear by April 30, 2007, I will be forced to deal with you in Small Claims Court.

Sincerely,

Julie Gardner

Many of my students have written such letters to people who had "ripped them off," and they have received payment. Most people and companies do not want to be taken to court. A book that guided me through this process is called *Everybody's Guide to Small Claims Court* by Ralph Warner, who is an attorney.

Exercise
Write a formal letter of warning to sue someone or a company. Discuss.

Résumés and Job Applications

Résumés are very tricky. The applicant is attempting to impress the readers that she is best for the job and deserves an interview. Don't do like I have done in the past, and go overboard. Send just what is asked of you; no more, no less. I was recently advised to send my complete bio and backup information, and I did not get the interview. When I send only what is asked of me, I get the interview every time. Getting the job is a separate challenge, but first, your application process must get you in the door.

Follow the instructions the business gives on their application information accurately. I even put my paperwork in the same order that the business requests.

Exercise
List some things that you would like in your letter of interest, then write the letter. Refer to the example below, which is a letter of interest to a campus where I was already teaching part time Discuss.

Sample letter of interest

Universal Image Production
Marcielle Brandler
Address

City, CA 90000   Telephone & Fax
                                        marcielle@xxx.x

_____

_____ College
Attn: Human Resources
Street address
City, state zip

April 1, 2007

Dear Human Resources and Hiring Committee:

I am enclosing my résumé and other important papers to apply for the full-time, tenure-track teaching position at _____ College. I have been teaching English part-time at _____ since the fall of 2000 and at LA City College since spring 1988.

I enjoy teaching at _____, and I believe I am a favorite among students, because I conduct my classes in such a way as to instill in them confidence. I also give them the tools they need for critical thinking and writing. In class discussions, we compare examples from the required stories and articles to present-day issues we face as a culture and as individuals. I think of teaching as my mission and as an honor. I am happy at _____ in my part-time position and would like to participate in the larger decision-making role of planning curricula, helping to design exciting learning environments, and having my own office space with office hours.

Having been on the boards of a few organizations has taught me the value of working with others towards specific, obtainable goals. As a published writer, I can help with writers' competitions. I have been a judge for the LA City College contest in poetry for two years. I have also organized, advertised, and hosted events for organizations since 1982, which I can do at our campus. I have also taught Poetry Workshops since 1986 with California Poets in the Schools.

I look forward to working with the faculty and staff at _____ in a more in-depth manner, if I am hired for this position. Please feel free to contact me at any time.

Thank you.

Sincerely,

Marcielle Brandler

Be sure to sign the letter. Many department chairs and business owners tell me that people forget to sign their letters, and the signature makes it a legal document. Notice that I mention the name of my prospective campus several times. I want them to know that it is *their* campus at which I wish to teach, and not just a random place. I want to avoid making it look like a form letter.

Exercise
Create a letter of interest for yourself. Discuss.

Create a Letterhead
A letterhead is the top information which the reader can use to contact you. I would not place it at the bottom of the letter, because most people look at the top. Do that for all formal letters.

Exercise
Create a letterhead for yourself. Discuss.

Avoid adjectives praising yourself. Do not say, for example, "I know I will be a great teacher," or "People say I do a fabulous job." Instead, say exactly what you have done, and state it as a simple fact. For example, "I was top sales representative for five years." If you can, give the exact title. This makes it more formal and matter of fact. I was skating on the edge of this idea when I wrote: "I believe I am a favorite among students, because I conduct my classes in such a way as to instill in them confidence." However, I did follow it with actual facts: "I also give them the tools they need for critical thinking and writing. In class discussions, we compare examples from the required stories and articles to present-day issues we face as a culture and as individuals."

The Résumé
Again, these letters are tricky. It is often a great idea to pay someone to help format your résumé and letter. A college student showed me his résumé, which listed only one thing. I asked him to tell me about some of the things he did in his community and some of the little jobs at which he had worked. From this information, we created a substantial résumé for him. We enhanced it with true accomplishments. He was proud to show it to perspective clients. Below is an edited selection from my résumé with some information purposely omitted:

Marcielle Brandler	Email address
Address	Phone
City, state zip code	www.website.com

Objective
Seeking a position as full-time and/or tenure-track English instructor

Job Titles
Associate professor, _____ College District
College instructor, lecturer, poetry workshop director, grammar instructor/mentor

Poetry mentor, award-winning poet, author
Public speaker, seminar director, events organizer/host

Skills

Instructor for English composition, critical thinking, grammar, and literature courses
Instructor for English as a second language
Creative writing instructor (poetry)
Events organizer/host.

Degrees

1994 Master of professional writing, MPW/MFA. University ____, city, state.
1981 Bachelor of arts, English. University ___ city, state.

Positions Occupied

1988–present. Create and direct poetry workshops. Mentored younger poet through ____ Academy for third-grade classes.

1988–present. English composition instructor, part-time. ___ College, city, state. English 103, 101, 21, & 28. Lecturer. Teach Critical Thinking.

1996. Poetry workshop director. Grades 4–6, ___ Elementary School, city, state.

1995. English instructor, part-time. ___ College, city, state.

Certificates and Credentials

___ Community College Credential, April 1990. Valid for Life.
___ University Transcript, September 1995. Prague Summer Writing Program.
___ College Writers' Day Festival, 1997. First prize for poem, "Eden."
___ College Academic Rank of Adjunct Associate Professor, October 2009.

Professional and Other Memberships

California Poets in the Schools, member since 1986.
California Teachers' Association, member since 1988.

Publications: Books, CD's, and DVD's

The Breathing House: Imagist Poems, by Marcielle Brandler, available on Amazon.com & Borders Bookstores, published 2006 by iUniverse.com.

The Breathing House, a CD of poems with a soundtrack engineered by Harlan Collins and produced by Chris LePlus. www.rhapsody.com/marciellebrandler/thebreathinghouse.

News Media and Articles by Marcielle

"Bury Me in Mojave" (poem), *America Anthology*, December 2009.

"Garden of Life" (article), *Science of Mind Magazine*, January 2010, page 106.

"Mind Control," *Religion & Ethics Digest*, 1995.

"Complain Drain," *Religion & Ethics Digest*, 1995.

Columnist, *Creative Line* (Glenn Horton), 2003.

"The Civilian, The Siege" (poem) was praised by *LA Weekly*'s Evelyn McDonnell, as one of the best in the CD anthology *Disclosure*.

"Mobile Poets Using Talents to Aid Homeless," People section, *Pasadena Star News*, January 22, 1986.

Television and Radio

Interview with Verbon Kelley, *Spotlight WKRE Blues Revue*, XRadio, October 2, 2006.

"Guest, Poet Marcielle Brandler," *Spending a Little Time with Poetry*, TV show produced and hosted by Bozana Belokosa, 2009.

"Guest, Poet Marcielle Brandler," *Laff It Off with Grace*, with host/comedian Grace Fraga, Comcast Public Access Television, Eagle Rock, CA, 2007.

Marcielle Presents! interview and arts public access television show, Pasadena Community Network, Pasadena, CA (formerly at Adelphia Studios, then Comcast Studios in Eagle Rock, CA), 2005 to present.

"Guests, Marcielle Brandler and Bonita Bradley," *Poetry Night Live with host, Myron Ruderman*, Tujunga Cable Television, Tunjunga, CA, 1986.

Web Pages

To hear and read Marcielle's poetry : www.audiolunchbox.com.

Marcielle Presents!: www.marciellepresents.com.

Fun with Grammar: http://yvonne333.wordpress.com.

Universal Image Productions, an educational site: www.webspawner.com/users/marcielle.

Member webpage at Alameda Writers' Group website: www.alamedawritersgroup.org.

Laff It Off with Grace: http://video.google.com/videoplay?docid=-8130130549306438467#
.

Exercise

Create a short résumé for yourself. Discuss.

Lying on Résumés

Lying or bending the truth on résumés or on any correspondence is not acceptable. No matter what others do, remain blameless and have an absolutely clear conscience. Even when you believe that others succeeded because of their lies, continue on your honest path.

Letters of Reference

Have the courage to ask your boss, department chair, or client for a letter of reference. All he or she can do is refuse. Many people also post films on our websites like You Tube showing clients praising their work. When requesting a reference, be sure to ask only people who you know feel good about you. Also read the letter and check it for anything that might hint of condescension.

I was once given a letter of reference from the chair of the English department at a high school where I had taught. She wrote, "Marcielle has finally settled down ..." I never used that letter; the lady knew nothing about my personal life and did not know if I had "settled down" or not.

Often, you will be asked to write some ideas for the letter. Do this even if you are not asked. Write in your e-mail or note to the person, "Thank you for agreeing to write this letter. Here is a reminder of some of the things you might want to cover: I created a new filing system, which is currently being used. I sold over $100,000 worth of product," etc. People forget about the accomplishments of others, so help them remember the highlights, the ones that are the most impressive.

Below is a note I wrote to my Dean of Academic Affairs who was willing to write me a letter of recommendation.

April 6, 2010

Hi, P___:
Thanks for doing this. Some ideas are below.

To Whom it May Concern:

I am writing this letter as a recommendation for Marcielle Brandler, who has been teaching English composition, literature, and critical thinking here at _____ College since 2000. Many students who take her developmental writing courses sign up for her more advanced classes.

Marcielle's genuine excitement for her subject matter infuses students with that same passion. During class discussions and group work, she is able to get students to think about the ethical and social issues raised in the required readings. This passion then moves into their own work. She encourages them to get extra help in the Writing Center, and she sets aside special times to work with each student personally. She has developed a "Partner Sheet" that students use to do peer work on essays.

her goal is to see every one of them succeed in her class and to resolve any personal issues that may block their college progress.

Marcielle works well with colleagues and is good at problem solving. She would be an excellent addition to any campus community.

That is all I could think of. Feel free to use any part of or all of the above "letter." Thanks so much.

Marcielle

I was very happy with what he wrote for me and am proud to use that letter in my resume packet.

Exercise
Write a letter of reference for yourself or someone else. Discuss.

Do your research. Find out what you can about the organization and how you might fit in, whether you have something to offer. I do not try to find out what sport the hiring person likes or anything like that. I am just myself and as genuine as I can be. It's also important to look around and see the mood of the place. Is this a place you would want to spend time? Talk to people. Get a feel for them.

Application Letters to Colleges and Universities
Students believe that they have to list all of their accomplishments to impress the officials at the college they wish to attend. Colleges also want diversity, so the things that make you different from other prospective students might benefit you. If you are from Barbados and your father was a poor farmer who came here with $10 and became a citizen, that might be something the application readers want to see. Since I am no expert in this, consult college administrators and guidance counselors, and search on the Internet for advice. A simple phone call or e-mail will suffice. Be clear about what advice you seek.

The essay should include some highlights about yourself. List what you have done, no matter how small it seems to be. Possible accomplishments include church activities and tutoring. Describing your skills, such as math, gardening, writing, singing, etc., is also helpful. Write about what these jobs have taught you and explain why you want to go to this particular college/university and what you will contribute and study. Describe what you plan to do for your livelihood when you graduate.

Exercise
Write an application letter to a college or university. Make one up or use an existing one for which you would like help. Discuss.

Business Letters

Business letters should be formal, concise, clear, and polite. Just like the letter to sue, state what you want and why. The letter below notifies the company that I would like the money they charged me for their product to be reimbursed to my credit card. I copied their invoice into the letter, as evidence and for their convenience.

Marcielle Brandler
Address   Telephone & Fax
City, CA 90000   marcielle@verizon.net

___ Technologies, USA, Inc.
Customer Service
Address
City, state, zip

Dear Customer Service Dept:

I called your phone number at 866-_____ and went to the proper exten-
sion, #2 which is supposed to be for "personal computer support," but was
kicked off the system several times. I have deleted this security program
from my system, since there is no e-mail, chat, or phone help available.
Please reimburse my credit card for any charges. I have enclosed a record of
my transactions for your convenience. I do not feel I should have to make
a phone call for which I will be charged, as with your 978 area code phone
number listed. My "Windows cannot load Internet Explorer," says the computer.

___ would not let me get on the Internet, and now, even though I have un-
installed it, my ability to get into Internet Explorer seems to be permanently
damaged. I went to www.___Support and got nothing and to 855 _____
phone number.

I need the Internet for my teaching. This is very frustrating. If you can offer
any help, I would appreciate it. ___ (my provider) tried to fix it and failed.
See attached receipt.

Sincerely,

Marcielle Brandler

The company reimbursed my money within a few days.

Exercise

Write a letter to a business from whom you would like help or correction for services or a
product. Make one up, or rework an existing one. Discuss.

Phone Calls

Phone calls are a more personal and direct way to reach someone, but there is no paper trail with which to keep a record. However, a person can keep a phone log of calls, if need be.

Most people know that phone etiquette for business means that the conversation needs to be polite, short, direct, and clear. Some people ramble on an on, but most know that we are all busy and do not have time to chat for long periods of time.

I often write down what was said in a phone call when I know that I may need to refer to that information later. An example is below. This is an e-mail I sent in 2009 regarding a phone call about accepting a teaching assignment:

> Dear Help Desk at Human Resources:
>
> I did accept the class offered to me, so I would like to have the R (Refused) listing on the Seniority List changed.
>
> I called six times within two weeks to accept the class that was offered for Spring 09, but no one called back to confirm, so I was forced to accept a class elsewhere at the same time.
> Please change the R to something more accurate.
>
> Thank you,
>
> Marcielle Brandler
> Sept. 28, 2009

E-mails

E-mails are considered legal documents in courts. Be careful about what you say in any e-mail, even those which you think are private. When e-mailing someone you do not know, do what you would do in a letter, and address that person by her formal name.

> June 21, 2011
>
> Dear Mrs. Samuelson:
>
> Thank you for giving me the information I need to apply for the teaching job. I will mail my package to Human Resources tomorrow.
>
> I appreciate all your help.
>
> Thank you.
>
> Melinda Parks

If you are requesting something, be brief and clear. Leave your contact information and a time that you will call the person for further confirmation. Save all your important e-mails in a special document or folder that you can access when you need to.

Exercise
Write an e-mail to someone. Make one up or rework an existing one. Discuss.

Critical Thinking

Critical thinking is deep consideration of an issue or information presented dispassionately, meaning without personal biases. We must be willing to set aside our personal prejudices and allow only the evidence to influence us. This is difficult for many people. They cannot separate themselves from their beliefs and entertain another person's point of view. This is a skill we must strive toward.

The *Critical Thinking Community* website says the following:

> Critical thinking is the intellectually disciplined process of actively and skillfully conceptualizing, applying, analyzing, synthesizing, and/or evaluating information gathered from, or generated by, observation, experience, reflection, reasoning, or communication, as a guide to belief and action. In its exemplary form, it is based on universal intellectual values that transcend subject matter divisions: clarity, accuracy, precision, consistency, relevance, sound evidence, good reasons, depth, breadth, and fairness. It entails the examination of those structures or elements of thought implicit in all reasoning: purpose, problem, or question-at-issue, assumptions, concepts, empirical grounding; reasoning leading to conclusions, implications and consequences, objections from alternative viewpoints, and frame of reference. Critical thinking—in being responsive to variable subject matter, issues, and purposes—is incorporated in a family of interwoven modes of thinking, among them: scientific thinking, mathematical thinking, historical thinking, anthropological thinking, economic thinking, moral thinking, and philosophical thinking.

> Critical thinking can be seen as having two components: a set of skills to process and generate information and beliefs, and the habit, based on intellectual commitment, of using those skills to guide behavior. It is thus to be contrasted with: the mere acquisition and retention of information alone (because it involves a particular way in which information is sought and treated), the mere possession of a set of skills (because it involves the continual use of them), and the mere use of those skills ("as an exercise") without acceptance of their results.

> Critical thinking varies according to the motivation underlying it. When grounded in selfish motives, it is often manifested in the skillful manipulation

of ideas in service to one's own, or one's groups', vested interest. As such, it is typically intellectually flawed, however pragmatically successful it might be. When grounded in fair mindedness and intellectual integrity, it is typically of a higher order intellectually, though subject to the charge of "idealism" by those habituated to its selfish use.

Critical thinking of any kind is never universal in any individual; everyone is subject to episodes of undisciplined or irrational thought. Its quality is therefore usually a matter of degree and dependent on, among other things, the quality and depth of experience in a given domain of thinking or with respect to a particular class of questions. No one is a critical thinker through-and-through, but only to such-and-such a degree, with such-and-such insights and blind spots, subject to such-and-such tendencies towards self-delusion. For this reason, the development of critical thinking skills and dispositions is a lifelong endeavor.

-"Defining Critical Thinking"

Exercise

Choose a newspaper article and answer the questions below. This assignment is designed to assess your critical-thinking, problem-solving, and communication skills. Your answer will be judged for clarity, relevance, coherence, logic, depth, consistency, and fairness. More specifically, the reader will be asking the following questions:

Is the question at issue well stated? Is it clear and unbiased? Does the expression of the question do justice to the complexity of the matter at issue?

Does the writer cite relevant evidence, experiences, and information essential to the issue?

Does the writer clarify key concepts when necessary?

Does the writer show a sensitivity to what he is assuming or taking for granted (as far as those assumptions might reasonably questioned)?

Does the writer develop a definite line of reasoning, explaining well how he or she is arriving at his or her conclusions?

Is the writer's reasoning well supported?

Does the writer show a sensitivity to alternative points of view or lines of reasoning? Does he consider and respond to objections framed from other points of view?

Does the writer show a sensitivity to the implications and consequences of the position he or she has taken?

Logical Fallacies

Description of Fallacies

To understand what a fallacy is, one must understand what an argument is. Briefly, an argument consists of one or more premises and one conclusion. A premise is a statement that is either true or false offered in support of the claim being made, which is the conclusion (also a sentence that is either true or false).

There are two main types of arguments: deductive and inductive. A deductive argument is an argument such that the premises provide (or appear to provide) complete support for the conclusion. An inductive argument is an argument in which the premises provide (or appear to provide) less than complete support for the conclusion. If the premises actually provide the required degree of support for the conclusion, then the argument is a good one. A good deductive argument is known as a valid argument; if all its premises are true, then its conclusion must be true. If all the argument is valid and has all true premises, then it is a sound argument. If it is invalid or has one or more false premises, it will be unsound. A good inductive argument is known as a strong (or "cogent") inductive argument: if most of the premises are true, the conclusion is likely to be true.

A fallacy is, very generally, an error in reasoning. This differs from a factual error, which is simply being wrong about the facts. To be more specific, a fallacy is an "argument" in which the premises given for the conclusion do not provide the needed degree of support. A deductive fallacy is a deductive argument that is invalid (it is such that it could have all true premises and still have a false conclusion). An inductive fallacy is less formal than a deductive fallacy. They are simply "arguments" which appear to be inductive arguments, but the premises do not provided enough support for the conclusion. In such cases, even if the premises were true, the conclusion would not be more likely to be true.

Examples of Fallacies

Inductive argument
Premise 1: Most American cats are domestic house cats.
Premise 2: Bill is an American cat.
Conclusion: Bill is domestic house cat.

Factual error
Columbus is the capital of the United States.

Deductive fallacy
Premise 1: If Portland is the capital of Maine, then it is in Maine.
Premise 2: Portland is in Maine.
Conclusion: Portland is the capital of Maine.
(Portland is the largest city in Maine, but Augusta is the capital.)

Inductive Fallacy
Premise 1: Having just arrived in Ohio, I saw a white squirrel.
Conclusion: All squirrels in Ohio are white.
(While there are many squirrels in Ohio, the white ones are very rare.)

See "Fallacies" in the "Works Cited" section.

Exercise
Create or find a logical fallacy, and discuss its problems.

Afterword

This is the end of Marcielle Brandler's first grammar book. Look for more in the future. I hope you have enjoyed this journey through the English language. Please check out the sources below. They have been handpicked and are excellent places to visit. Happy learning!

Works Cited

Bookgrl [pseud.]. "Hillary Clinton Facing Undiscussed Sexism." *MDD: My Direct Democracy*, December 2, 2007. Accessed June 29, 2011. http://mydd.com/users/bookgrl/posts/hillary-clinton-facing-undiscussed-sexism.

Brandler, Marcielle. "Enigmatic Emperors," review of *The Emperor's Club. . Universal Image Productions.* Accessed April 4, 2011. www.webspawner.com/users/marcielle/filmreviewofemp.html.

 "Salma Kahlo," review of *Frida. Universal Image Productions.* Accessed April 4, 2011. www.webspawner.com/users/marcielle/filmreviewoffri.html.

"Chicago-Style Citation Quick Guide." *Chicago Manual of Style.* Accessed Dec 25, 2011. http://www.chicagomanualofstyle.org/home.html

"Defining Critical Thinking." *The Critical Thinking Community.* 2011. Accessed June 27, 2011. www.criticalthinking.org/aboutCT/define_critical_thinking.cfm.

"Difference Between Works Cited and Bibliography." *DifferenceBetween.net*, 2011. www.differencebetween.net/language/difference-between-works-cited-and-bibliography. Accessed May 3, 2011. Used with permission.

"Diphthongs." *Can Do's Helper Page*, October 26, 2008. Accessed July 1, 2011. http://rbeaudoin333.homestead.com/diphthong_1.html.

Fearon, B. L. "Dipthongs and Digraphs." *PhonicsWorld.com*, 2004–6. Accessed April 14, 2011. www.phonicsworld.com/voweldiphthong.html. Used with author's permission.

Gipson, Fred. *Old Yeller.* New York: Harper & Row Publishers, 1956.

Harper, Douglas. "Hanged." In *Online Etymology Dictionary*, 2001–10. www.etymonline.com.

Healy, Mellissa. "A Plant-based Diet. Less Salt. More Exercise," *Los Angeles Times* "Health" section, June 28, 2010.

"Jihad: Supreme Efforts in the Way of Allah." Guidance from the Holy Qur'an. *Al Islam. The Official Website of the Ahmadiyya Muslim Community*, 1995–2011. Accessed June 27, 2011. www.alislam.org/jihad/quran.html.

Labossiere, Michael C. "Constructing a Logical Argument," 1997Acessed December 25, 2011. http://www.infidels.org/library/modern/mathew/logic.html. (With permission)

Labossiere, Michael C. "Fallacies." *The Nizkor Project*, 1995. www.nizkor.org/features/fallacies. (with permission)

"New Research: Substantial Wrinkle Reduction Now Possible with Topical Creams." *BeautyUser.com*. Accessed May 3, 2011. www.beautyuser.com.

Owens, Kevin. "Digraphs." *PhonicsOntheWeb*, 2006. Accessed July 1, 2011. www.phonicsontheweb.com/digraphs.php.

"Philistine." In *Dictionary.com*, 2011. Accessed April 30, 2011. http://dictionary.reference.com.

"PhilistineQuotes." *SearchQuotes*, 2011. Accessed September 10, 2011. www.searchquotes.com/search/?searchf=philistine&sbut.x=0&sbut.y=0.

"Phonics." *MES English. Free Printables for Teachers*, 2005–11. Accessed June 29, 2011. www.mes-english.com/phonics.php.

Polite English, 2003–11. Accessed June 29, 2011. http://polite-english.com.

Setchfield, Kristopher. "Is Masauru Emoto for Real?!! Are Dr. Masaru Emoto's Fantastic Claims Actually Real?" December 20, 2005. Accessed July 5, 2011. www.is-masaru-emoto-for-real.com. (With author's permission).

Uittenbogaard, Arie. "Meaning and etymology of the name Palestine (Philistia, Philistine, Philistines)." *Meaning and Etymology of Bible Names*. Abarim Publications, 2000–2011. Accessed April 30, 2011. www.abarim-publications.com/Meaning/Palestine.html. Reprinted with permission from the author.

"Using Concrete Nouns." *ChangingMinds.org*, 2002–11. Accessed November 21, 2011. http://changingminds.org/techniques/language/speech_parts/concrete_nouns.htm.

"Works Cited, References, and Bibliography: What's the Difference?" *A Research Guide for Students*. 1998–2008. Accessed May 3, 2011. www.aresearchguide.com/10works.html.

Vasquez, B., D. Fuhrmann, and A. Mezyn. "MLA (Modern Language Association) Style—Citing Online Sources." *Los Angeles City College Study Aid*. Los Angeles: Martin Luther King Jr. Library, Los Angeles City College, 2009. Accessed June 27, 2011. www.lacitycollege.edu/resource/library/LibraryInstruction/HANDOUT_MLA_Online%207th%20ed%2009_2009.pdf. 27 June 2011.

Suggested Resources

Abacus Educational Services. Accessed June 20, 2011. http://abacus-es.com.

Diana Hacker publishes a very popular book, *Rules for Writers*, that is required at many colleges and universities. Her website has very good exercises and more: www.DianaHacker.com.

Modern Language Association, 2011. Accessed 19, 2011. www.mla.org/homepage.

Purdue University has a very comprehensive site:

Marcielle Brandler

Purdue Online Writing Lab, 1995–2011. http://owl.english.purdue.edu/owl.

Schachter, Norman, and Alfred T. Clark. *English the Easy Way.* Los Angeles: Southwestern Publishing Co., 1985.

Talib, Ismail S. "Looking at Nouns, Verbs and Other Simple Constituents." *Literary Stylistics: Lecture Notes #2*, December 25, 2010. Accessed April 24, 2011. http://courses.nus.edu.sg/course/ellibst/lsl02.html#abstract_noun.

Warner, Ralph. *Everybody's Guide to Small Claims Court.* Berkeley: Nolo Publishing, 2010.

Author's Biography

Marcielle Brandler appears in *Who's Who in the World*. She obtained her Master's degree in Professional Writing and poetry in 1994. A former singer/songwriter, her poetry is lyrical and sensual. Her poems have been translated into Czech, French, Arabic, and Spanish and have been published all over the world. *The Breathing House*, a book of her poems, was published in 2006. Her poem "Eden" won first place at the Mt. San Antonio College's 1997 Writers' Day Festival. "The Civilian, The Siege" was praised by *LA Weekly*'s Evelyn McDonnell as one of the best in the CD anthology *Disclosure*. She has been organizing poetry events and workshops since the early 1980s to benefit various organizations, including her own group Urban Mobile Poets and the Literacy Campaign. In December 2009, her poem titled "Bury Me in Mojave" was published in *America Anthology* and her article "Garden of Life" was published in the January 2010 issue of *Science of Mind*, just to mention a few She is also a speaker, seminar director, filmmaker, and Associate Professor.

Marcielle teaches college-level English, and her *Fun with Grammar* website is for students, educators, and scholars looking for advice on grammar, literature, writing, and anything to do with the English language. She has been an entertainment writer for *Sierra Madre Vista* and *Creative Line Magazine*, and a writer for *Religion & Ethics Digest*. She was a featured poet at Universita Karlova (Charlse University) and Radost in Prague, Czech Republic, and an associate producer for the film *The Last Weekend*, which aired on Lifetime television.

Marcielle can be reached at marcielle@verizon.net or via her websites at:
Educational site. www.webspawner.com/users/marcielle
Fun with Grammar site. http://yvonne333.wordpress.com/